When Life
Gives You
PINEAPPLES,
Make an
Upside-down
Cake!

When Life Gives You PINEAPPLES, Make an Upside-down Cake!

*Wisdom and Daily Devotions
by Fr. Dale Fushek
with Jody Serey and Friends*

This devotional is dedicated to all who struggle to find God in our daily lives. We offer a profound "thank you" to the people of the Praise and Worship Center for their contributions to this book.

Thank you to artist, Elaine Dube, from the Praise and Worship Center, for the gift of the cover art. Thank you to David Serey, Peter Rehm-Gerdes, and Stephanie Rehm for their assistance in production.

May this devotional find a way to the bedside of each person who is seeking a deeper daily walk with God.

Fr. Dale Fushek
Jody Serey

ISBN: 978-1-881276-22-7

Web site: pwcdevotionals.com

January 1

ONE LESSON I HAVE LEARNED IN MY LIFE IS...

God likes new beginnings! How do I know? Every day, He gives us a new sunrise. Every time we ask, He gives us forgiveness. Every moment He gives us the grace and courage we need to make better and healthier choices.

Today is New Year's Day. We have the opportunity to start fresh again. This day should be filled with hope, new possibilities, and an awareness that this year can be better than last year.

Hopelessness, depression, regret, and guilt never help. But the God of sunrises, mercy, and fresh beginnings helps tremendously.

PRAYER FOR THE BLESSING OF THE DAY...

Lord, on this New Year's Day, I ask You to make my heart brand new. Don't let me be stuck in the past, but through Your kindness, grant me a freshness of spirit. Bless my family, my church, my friends, and my nation. Bless this New Year, dear God, and make it a year of amazing spiritual growth. AMEN.

Fr. Dale

January 2

ONE LESSON I HAVE LEARNED IN MY LIFE IS...

Few things in life are as scary as the container of gravy that got lost in the back of the refrigerator on Thanksgiving.

PRAYER FOR THE BLESSING OF THE DAY...

Lord, it is day two of another year, and already I am encountering the problems of the year just gone by. Please help me remember that every morning is a new day, and every dawn brings with it renewed opportunities to be useful, bring joy, and encounter mercy.

Jody Serey

January 3

ONE LESSON I HAVE LEARNED IN MY LIFE IS...

I want to give my life to God. And I have also learned that it is not an easy thing to do. Every time I pray the Our Father, I mean the words "thy will be done." But, moments later, I am already wanting my life and my wants to go my WAY.

The great spiritual writer C.S. Lewis said, "The terrible thing, the almost impossible thing, is to hand over your whole self -- all your wishes and precautions to Christ. Until you have given up yourself to Him, you will not have a real self." I hope today, and in this coming year, to find my true self.

PRAYER FOR THE BLESSING OF THE DAY...

Father, I give You my life. Let today be different than most days by helping me be faithful to my decision to abandon myself to You. Today, Lord, help me to live no longer to myself, but for You. AMEN.

Fr. Dale

January 4

ONE LESSON I HAVE LEARNED IN MY LIFE IS...

If you pull up to an elementary school while doing the song/dance "Whip and Nae Nae", your 10 year old daughter will run out of your car quickly. There is a time your children adore you...then a time they think you are weird...then a time they may hate you...but there will be a time they love and adore you again.

PRAYER FOR THE BLESSING OF THE DAY...

God, help me do the things I need to do.

Erika Kieny Broderson

January 5

ONE LESSON I HAVE LEARNED IN MY LIFE IS...

Everyone tells me I need to surrender to God's will, but no one really tells us how to do that. I recently read some helpful hints from Pastor Rick Warren. One of the things he says about surrender is "waiting for God's timing without knowing when it will come." I think that is profound. Most of us intellectually know that God cares for us. But, we want Him to act on our time-table. God doesn't do that. He doesn't take away the freedom or the choices that people in my life choose to make. And he doesn't take away my freedom, either. But rather, He is a patient God who can take a bad situation and turn it into something life-giving. There are many times in my life I did not understand how God was working. But, when I look back, I can see He was. Our God is worthy of our TRUST, our CONFIDENCE, and our HOPE.

PRAYER FOR THE BLESSING OF THE DAY...

Jeremiah 29:11

"For surely I know the plans I have for you, says the Lord, plans for your welfare and not for your harm, to give you a future with hope." I trust You, Lord. AMEN.

Fr. Dale

January 6

ONE LESSON I HAVE LEARNED IN MY LIFE IS...

Home spun wisdom is sometimes much greater than that of the great philosophers. Former major league baseball player Yogi Berra recently died. He was famous for his quotes. Even though he said "I never said most of the things I said", he sure said some great things. The truest thing he said was "It isn't over till it's over".

My younger brother was told he had about six months to live. He had been hit very hard with hepatitis C. A new treatment came out recently. After six months he has been declared "cured" by the doctors at St. Joseph's Hospital.

As you can imagine, my family is delighted. Sometimes life takes twists and turns we aren't expecting. In this case, it was a miracle.

I know that life isn't meant to go on forever. I also know that many folks never receive a cure they pray for, and not every story has a happy ending. But, it's good to remember, that "nothing is over until it's over." So hope is always a good option.

PRAYER FOR THE BLESSING OF THE DAY....

Lord, be with all those who feel hopeless today. Give us the grace to know that all of our hope needs to be in YOU and in Your mercy. AMEN.

Fr. Dale

January 7

ONE LESSON I HAVE LEARNED IN MY LIFE IS...

There is way too much DRAMA. Drama, to me, includes over-reading into situations, making something not about you, to be about you, and being offended when no offense was meant. Some folks thrive in drama. It certainly makes good TV. But, it doesn't make a happy life environment for relationships to grow.

I try to not be a DRAMA king (or queen). But, I know I have my moments. I think we all need to work hard to not react to others who cause drama and to do our part in not creating it!

PRAYER FOR THE BLESSING OF THE DAY...

Lord, may I be so focused on You today, that I don't have the time or energy to create a response to drama. Help me Lord, to create a "drama free zone" around my life today. AMEN.

Fr. Dale

January 8

ONE LESSON I HAVE LEARNED IN MY LIFE IS...

Don't love someone who only sees you as an option.

Talk to people if you have problems on your mind; don't keep them in and let them sit.

Think of the consequences before you take action.

Give yourself alone time so you can dwell and think about yourself instead of being busy and dealing with other people's problems.

Keep your friends close to you and don't let them drift away. The more people you have to support you and talk to you, the better.

PRAYER FOR THE BLESSING OF THE DAY...

Lord, let people know that whatever they are going through, they are not alone. Fill us with Your love. AMEN.

Tristan Shepherd

January 9

ONE LESSON I HAVE LEARNED IN MY LIFE IS...

The one evening I say "I'll put gas in the car in the morning" is the beginning of the night that will find me making an emergency trip somewhere at 2:00 a.m. praying for something to be open.

PRAYER FOR THE BLESSING OF THE DAY...

Lord, we are often unprepared for the roads we must take. Please be our eyes when we must find our way in the dark, and guide us on unfamiliar highways through life. And when we reach our destination, help us remember to be grateful for the journey and our companions along the way.

Jody Serey

January 10

ONE LESSON I HAVE LEARNED IN MY LIFE IS...

Prayer and praise bring me closer to the Lord and allow me to hear His voice in my life. Prayer can be a community effort and prayer can be an extremely personal communication with God the Father, God the Son, and God the Holy Spirit. God is always there to hear our call. He loves to be in connection with us. I've discovered that I don't need fancy words to talk to my God; I just need to share my heart. I let His spirit guide my prayers. I try to begin with a thank you and then have a conversation with the One who loves me so. At times, all I can do is plead, "I need You, God" or "Lord, help me!" He knows my heart and is there waiting for me to connect with Him. I try to offer each of my days as a prayer of thanks for all my blessings. I also do my very best

5

to talk with Him and listen to Him each day. I have to remember to listen and not to just pour out my needs so that I can hear/sense/experience His will for my life and His direction for my issues. I've learned that He hears and answers me even when I'm not attentive to my relationship with Him. I know that when I am attentive to my relationship with Him that I walk with much more peace and wisdom and much closer to my God.

PRAYER FOR THE BLESSING OF THE DAY...

Heavenly Father,

Thank you for loving us and guiding us. You love to have us walk closely to You in all parts of our lives. Help us to grow more and more comfortable talking and connecting with You through prayer so that we walk more closely to You. Help us grow stronger in hearing You when You reach out to us. Help us walk each day in relationship with You. We pray this in the name of Jesus. AMEN.

Debbie Smith

January 11

ONE LESSON I HAVE LEARNED IN MY LIFE IS...

I used to be proud of my accomplishments and possessions and boast about them. I used to give my opinion and advice to anyone who would listen. Now, I've lived long enough to realize my pride has hindered, not helped me, in my relationships and spiritual growth.

God is slowly revealing to me areas of pride that need to be tamed. I need to pray daily for the Holy Spirit to prompt me quickly and help me "tame my tongue."

PRAYER FOR THE BLESSING OF THE DAY...

Who makes you different from anyone else?

What do you have that you did not receive?

And if you did receive it, why did you boast

As though you did not?

(1 Corinthians 4:7)

Suzanne Cline

January 12

ONE LESSON I HAVE LEARNED IN MY LIFE IS...

Just as the bible says, "The truth will set you free" (John 8:32). The more honest I have become with myself and with others, the more free I have become to be the person God made me to be.

A man named James Faust said, "Honesty is more than not lying. It is truth telling, truth speaking, truth living, and truth loving."

Here is a bit of truth for you. God is worthy of our worship and praise. And, here is another bit of truth. You and I need God in our lives.

PRAYER FOR THE BLESSING OF THE DAY...

Father, make this a day full of truth. Help me to be honest with myself and see the things I need to change in my life. Help me to become a truly FREE person...free to be ME...free to live...and FREE to PRAISE YOU.

As Matt Maher's song says, "Lord, I Need You." AMEN.

Fr. Dale

January 13

ONE LESSON I HAVE LEARNED IN MY LIFE IS...

Rich Mullins wrote the best lyrics of any Christian artist. Somehow he was able to capture feelings and thoughts like no one else. During the darkest times of my life, I clung onto some of Rich's music. In a song called "We Are Not As Strong As We Think We Are", Rich wrote, "It took the hand of God Almighty to part the waters of the sea, but it only took one little lie to separate you and me." In a song called, "The Love of God", Rich refers to God's love as, "the reckless raging fury that they call the love of God." Profound!

PRAYER FOR THE BLESSING OF THE DAY...

"Sometimes my life just don't make sense at all. When the mountains look so big, and my faith just seems so small. So hold me Jesus, 'cause I'm shaking like a leaf. You have been King of my glory. Won't you be my Prince of Peace." (Rich Mullins)

Fr. Dale

January 14

ONE LESSON I HAVE LEARNED IN MY LIFE IS....

Not to limit God. Recently NASA was super excited to announce they have found traces of water on Mars. That means there could be life there or perhaps life was on Mars at some point. Why should that shock us? We belong to God; God does not belong to us. He is much bigger, much more powerful, much more capable of loving than we could ever imagine. Why should we think that our planet, our universe, or even our imaginations should set a limit on God?

Christian singer Chris Tomlin recorded a song called "Indescribable." The words of the song say "Indescribable, Uncontainable…All powerful, untamable, awestruck we fall to our knees, You are amazing God." God is amazing. He creates everything out of nothing. Our job is to simply be in awe of God and offer as best we can fitting praise and worship. Tomlin sings "Incomparable, and Unchangeable, You see the depths of my heart and You love me the same." Our God is AMAZING!

PRAYER FOR THE BLESSING OF THE DAY....

Thank you, Father, Creator, for loving me. Thank you for life, for creation, for eternity. I praise You, Lord! AMEN.

Fr. Dale

January 15

ONE LESSON I HAVE LEARNED IN MY LIFE IS...

Hope is essential for every human being. In my book *The Unexpected Life* I wrote, "We need hope, and in order to truly have hope we have to have the courage to accept love. That is the battle that most of have our whole lives. We don't have the innocence or the guts to accept human or Divine Love."

Once we come to know God's unconditional love, there is no reason to have anything but HOPE. He will not let go of us. He will not abandon us. He will not let us become lost.

PRAYER FOR THE BLESSING OF THE DAY...

Father, my hope for today is that I will come to know Your love in a deeper way than ever before. Let my hope in You overshadow my sadness, my disappointments, and my lack of trust. I trust You, Jesus, with my life. AMEN.

Fr. Dale

January 16

ONE LESSON I HAVE LEARNED IN MY LIFE IS...

Sometimes justice and mercy cannot break bread at the same table.

PRAYER FOR THE BLESSING OF THE DAY...

Lord, help me remember that sometimes even if I have the right to do something, I should still refrain from acting. Remind me always to measure righteous indignation against my need to forgive. Help redirect my energy towards finding a solution, or at least finding a way to prevent more damage from occurring. Help me place a premium on being kind, and not on being right.

Jody Serey

January 17

ONE LESSON I HAVE LEARNED IN MY LIFE IS...

There are a lot of smart and holy people out there that I have never heard of....and it is time I open my mind and heart to what they have to say. One of those people is a pastor named A. W. Tozer. Every Protestant theology student knows of him. I never heard of him before.

Tozer was a pastor, preacher, and author who was born in 1897. He was born into complete poverty and educated himself through grade school, high school, and even college. He was made a pastor even though he had no formal training. He eventually received two honorary doctorates and wrote 40 books. He gave proceeds from his books to the poor.

Among the many topics Tozer wrote about, my favorite is worship. He said "I think we are going to have to restudy this whole teaching of the place of the Holy Spirit in the Church. If the life goes out of a man's body, he is said to be a corpse." He goes on to say "So it is in the Church. It is literally true that some churches are dead. The Holy Spirit has gone out of them and all you have left are the remains."

PRAYER FOR THE BLESSING OF THE DAY...

Father, today I pray for all the dead churches in our world. Please breathe the Spirit into them. I pray, too, for my own church. Make us alive in Your spirit." AMEN.

Fr. Dale

January 18

ONE LESSON I HAVE LEARNED IN MY LIFE IS...

One lesson I have learned in my life is that perspective is a wonderful thing. It makes you wonder what would happen if we all gave thanks for everything we have, instead of worrying about what we don't have. Appreciate every single thing you have, especially your friends. Life is too short and friends are too few. Just remember the words from Disney's "Toy Story" -- You've got a friend in me. When the road looks rough ahead and you're miles and miles from your nice warm bed, remember what your old pal said: You've got a friend in me.

These words may not have been spoken by Jesus, but they are so true. When you are down and out and you don't know which way to turn, remember you have a friend in Jesus. He will not abandon you or let you down -- so have faith in Jesus.

PRAYER FOR THE BLESSING OF THE DAY...

Thank You, Lord, for the friends You have given me. They look after me in difficult times, and make me laugh and cry at the same time. Thank you for everything that they are, and for all their gifts and talents, because without them I am nothing. I know, Lord, that You are my friend and my Savior and I may not always see that; but I know You will always be there for me. I just say Your name and You are with me. Thank you, Jesus, for being my friend.

John 15: 12-17

Weldon Turner

January 19

ONE LESSON I HAVE LEARNED IN MY LIFE IS...

Is that we all need to pray more! The truth is...a lot of us don't know how to pray. Jesus tried to teach us when He gave us the words of the Our Father. But, instead of learning from Him, we memorized the words and thought that would make us holy. But, it does not. The spiritual writer Richard Rohr said, "The most simple rule for good prayer is honesty and humility." God desires for us to be AUTHENTIC -- to be ourselves with Him. He doesn't care about rituals or words, He cares about our hearts. Every day we need to approach God being ourselves. We bring our sins, our fears, and our hopes to Him. He accepts us as we are!

PRAYER FOR THE BLESSING OF THE DAY...

Lord, I don't know how to pray. Sometimes, I barely know how to be myself. All I ask, Lord, is that I have the strength to be myself today and offer myself completely to You. AMEN.

Fr. Dale

January 20

ONE LESSON I HAVE LEARNED IN MY LIFE IS...

Whether it's dealing with everyday life or with people, I've found that my attitude sets the stage for success or failure, happiness or unhappiness. There are pros and cons, positive and negative in every aspect of life but how I view each situation is the key. If my focus is on the negative then I'm more likely to give up and not even try. In essence, I've just made excuses for why I can't do it. When I focus on the positive than all sorts of possibilities arise, ideas are flowing and I'm striving to make it happen.

When it comes to people, there are good and bad traits in all of us, so to expect perfection in anyone is not being realistic and can only lead to aggravation. I will see whatever I focus on. If I'm looking for the negative traits in someone then I will surely find them, and it will cause me to feel irritated and even helpless because I want to change their "bad" habits when they have no intention of changing. That's when I realize that I'm the one who needs to change. My attitude towards them needs to change to one of acceptance and love, and to focus on the good that they bring to the world and to my life. When I focus on their good traits, it gives me a sense of peace and happiness to have them in my life and I can truly enjoy their company.

PRAYER FOR THE BLESSING OF THE DAY...

Lord, I thank You for this day and all the challenges that it may bring. Please help me to keep my focus on You and guide me to do Your will. Help me to see others as You see them, to treat them with love, understanding and respect and to reserve judgment for You and You alone. I ask these things in Jesus' name. AMEN.

M.J. Broudy

January 21

ONE LESSON I HAVE LEARNED IN MY LIFE IS...

The Holy Spirit is alive and active. In the wonderful book, Primal, author Mark Batterson says, "Christianity was never intended to be a noun. And when we turn it into a noun, it becomes a turn off. Christianity was intended to be a verb. We've got to obey the promptings of the Holy Spirit."

Many of us allow our faith to become boring. We keep doing the same religious things over and over. But, when we follow the Spirit, we never know where God will lead us next. Faith becomes exciting again.

PRAYER FOR THE BLESSING OF THE DAY...

Come Holy Spirit, fill my day with Your presence. Let me be obedient to Your promptings. Please, Lord, let today be an exciting faith-filled day.

Fr. Dale

January 22

ONE LESSON I HAVE LEARNED IN MY LIFE IS...

Enjoy each and every day – it is a gift. Do not worry about yesterday. It is done; learn from it. Make amends and move on. Prepare yourself for tomorrow, but don't spend endless time worrying about what might happen.

PRAYER FOR THE BLESSING OF THE DAY...

Help me to see and appreciate the beauty in Your world, every day. Lead me to live a better life learning from my mistakes of yesterday. Give me peace. Remind me that I have control of my attitude. Help me to put my trust in You. In Jesus' Name, AMEN.

Gerry DeVille

January 23

ONE LESSON I HAVE LEARNED IN MY LIFE IS...

Not to let fear rule my life. In fall 2004 I gave up fear, officially, in an essay I wrote for a local newspaper that actually had a Religion Section in the paper every Saturday. (Wow, that seems like a long time ago. Not only the Religion Section but a regular, paper newspaper that most people had delivered to their driveways each day!) I was in the process of leaving the Roman Catholic Church and a community that I dearly loved. But the church used fear to control and hurt people and I could no longer with integrity attend nor work for such an organization. So I wrote a kind of manifesto declaring that I was "giving up fear...all fear except the fears a mother has for her children no matter how old they get." It's been more than 10 years since that declaration and I've stuck to it pretty well...taking chances, risking security and courageously facing consequences. I can say that though I probably have experienced fear since then, I have always remembered my pledge and I have never again let fear rule me, or my life or my decisions.

1 John 4:18 There is no fear in love. Rather perfect love casts out fear.

PRAYER FOR THE BLESSING OF THE DAY...

"Our deepest fear is not that we are inadequate. Our deepest fear is that we are powerful beyond measure. It is our light, not our darkness that most frightens us. We ask ourselves 'Who am I to be brilliant, gorgeous, talented, and fabulous?'

Actually, who are you not to be? You are a child of God. Your play-ing small does not serve the world. There is nothing enlightened about shrinking so that other people won't feel insecure around you. We are all meant to shine, as children do. We were born to make manifest the glory of God that is within us. It's not just in some of us; it's in every-one. And as we let our own light shine, we unconsciously give other people permission to do the same. As we are liberated from our own fear, our presence automatically liberates others."

(Marianne Williamson, A Return to Love: Reflections on the Principles of "A Course in Miracles")

Sue Ringler

January 24

ONE LESSON I HAVE LEARNED IN MY LIFE IS...

Seeing God in other people.

By watching a wife say a final loving goodbye to her husband of sixty years, parents devoting every ounce of energy to a special needs child, substance abuse being overcome when all looked hopeless, parents never "giving up" on a child – no matter what -- an eighty year old gentleman attending daily mass, a child being kind to a homeless man when his parents couldn't look in the man's direction.

PRAYER FOR THE BLESSING OF THE DAY...

Lord, as I begin the day, help me be keenly aware of Your presence everywhere I go and in everyone I meet. When the feeling of negativity sets in and I see the sadness when I'm out and about, remind me that there are unseen treasures in these challenging events. Make me ever mindful that You are in control of every situation so that I will never question Your righteousness. Allow me to see everyone through Your eyes as Your image and likeness, never questioning or being judgmen-tal. Walk side by side and guide me with Your grace and healing pres-ence every day. AMEN.

Anonymous

January 25

ONE LESSON I HAVE LEARNED IN MY LIFE IS...

The pages with the splatters in the old cookbook contain the best recipes. A cookbook in pristine condition is not to be trusted.

PRAYER FOR THE BLESSING OF THE DAY...

Lord, if I have enough food for two and a bowl to share it in, let me know that I am better off than many others in the world who are hungry and alone. Whether seated at a banquet table or on a rock by the side of the road, I look to You for the bread of life.

Jody Serey

January 26

ONE LESSON I HAVE LEARNED IN MY LIFE IS...

Check the pockets of the kid's jacket before you buy a new pair of mittens.

PRAYER FOR THE BLESSING OF THE DAY...

Lord, help me remember that sometimes what seems lost is just out of sight. Remind to look before I act, and to not assume that there will be no return of what I can't find. And – if something is, indeed gone – help me make enough of what is left behind.

Jody Serey

January 27

ONE LESSON I HAVE LEARNED IN MY LIFE IS...

What I can't control is none of my business. Some people may find this age of social media, high technology and instant worldwide exposure to news and events exciting and exhilarating. Some of us don't.

We're becoming a nation preoccupied with so many events going on simultaneously that we lose focus of what's important and what's not. We're losing the infrastructure of family and values. The news media blasts us with situations and events worldwide that instill fear, mistrust, prejudice and anxiety causing some of us despair and doubt.

Rather than succumb to outside events that I have no interest or control over, one option is to take a deep breath, close my eyes, focus on our Lord and trust in Him alone.

Nothing else is my business.

PRAYER FOR THE BLESSING OF THE DAY...

Lord, help me to seek You whenever I'm impacted by an event that troubles one. Help me put my faith and trust in You alone, as You are the only one in control.

Tom Cutrera

January 28

ONE LESSON I HAVE LEARNED IN MY LIFE IS...

Some messages you see written on a poster are true. Not all of them are true -- but some are. I recently saw a cool poster which read "I am in charge of how I feel today and I am choosing HAPPINESS."

We often see happiness as something that happens to us or is created by the circumstance of life. But it is a choice, and we do have the power to be happy despite our circumstances.

In a book called Happiness Is an Inside Job, John Powell, S.J. says "I believe God made us to be happy in this world and forever in the next." Powell lists out ten practices to be HAPPY. It would sure make this New Year better than last year if we all worked on these.

PRACTICE 1: We must accept ourselves as we are.

PRACTICE 2: We must accept full responsibility for our lives.

PRACTICE 3: We must try to fulfill our needs for relaxation, exercise, and nourishment.

PRACTICE 4: We must make our lives an act of love.

PRACTICE 5: We must stretch by stepping out of our comfort zones.

PRACTICE 6: We must learn to be "goodfinders."

PRACTICE 7: We must seek growth, not perfection.

PRACTICE 8: We must learn to communicate effectively.

PRACTICE 9: We must learn to enjoy the good things of life.

PRACTICE 10: We must make prayer a part of our daily lives.

PRAYER FOR THE BLESSING OF THE DAY...

Lord, happiness is knowing You...trusting You...loving You...and knowing I am unconditionally loved by YOU. AMEN.

Fr. Dale

January 29

ONE LESSON I HAVE LEARNED IN MY LIFE IS...

All people bleed. As a firefighter/ paramedic for more than 25 years, I have seen every kind of human suffering imaginable. Even though we look different, talk different, have different ideas or backgrounds...we are all people -- and all people bleed.

Injury and illness affect us all and it doesn't matter if we are rich, poor, powerful, young or old it's not something we can buy, negotiate or bully our way out of. Every one of us at some time in our life will have a health problem.

There's a kind of equality that comes with tragedy. When a person is suffering from injury or illness, no matter who it is, in that moment we all need the help and kindness of another person. This has taught me that while we are all different, in a very real way we are all in this together.

PRAYER FOR THE BLESSING OF THE DAY....

Lord, bless us with kindness and compassion when it's our turn to suffer from illness or injury; may we find others to help us in our struggle. Lay Your hands of healing and comfort on us. In a special way, bless those who dedicate their lives to helping others deal with injury and illness (paramedics, nurses, doctors, etc.).

And even though we are different in many ways, help us to remember we all bleed and to show others who are in need understanding and compassion. AMEN.

Captain Sue

January 30

ONE LESSON I HAVE LEARNED IN MY LIFE IS...

The small pleasures in life are what we remember later on. Warm socks, hot coffee, or a bird calling in the middle of the night – these are the treasures we store up.

PRAYER FOR THE BLESSING OF THE DAY...

Lord, strip the clutter from my hands so I can pick up what truly matters. Turn my face away from glitter and point it towards the glow of moonlight. Silence the clanging gongs so that Your whisper reaches me. Keep me plain, keep me simple, keep me true to You. AMEN.

Jody Serey

January 31

ONE LESSON I HAVE LEARNED IN MY LIFE IS...

Everyone can do "something beautiful for God."

That was the title of the first book that came out about Mother Teresa of Calcutta. It was written by a man named Malcolm Muggeridge. Malcolm was a non-believer from England who went to see if the stories about this nun were true. When he arrived, he found out that they were simply a shadow of the truth and that what she was doing was truly something unique. After that book came out, Mother Teresa became a household name.

I don't pretend that any of us reading this devotional will be the next Mother Teresa. But, we don't need to be. Mother said "Be kind and merciful. Let no one ever come to you without coming away better and happier. Be the living expression of God's kindness: kindness in your face, kindness in your eyes, kindness in your smile, kindness in your warm greeting."

In other words, we can do something beautiful for God every day in the simple kindness we show one another. We may think that simple acts of kindness don't change the world. But, they do, at least for the person who receives them.

PRAYER FOR THE BLESSING OF THE DAY...

From Mother Teresa

"God's spirit is in my heart, He has called me and set me apart,

This is what I have to do.

He sent me to give good news to the poor, Tell prisoners that they are prisoners, no more. Tell blind people they can see, and set the downtrodden free.

And go tell everyone the news that the kingdom of God has come."

AMEN.

Fr. Dale

February 1

ONE LESSON I HAVE LEARNED IN MY LIFE IS...

The Lord is always in control. When we depend on Him for guidance and wisdom, we are able to find peace on our journey. The Lord is always with us; we just need to be humble and be aware of His awesome presence.

PRAYER FOR THE BLESSING OF THE DAY...

Lord, help us to be open to Your awesome love. May we always give You thanks and praise in our daily walk through life.

Terry Burchett

February 2

ONE LESSON I HAVE LEARNED IN MY LIFE IS...

Communication between two people is not easy. Some people have trouble saying what is inside of them. They may have a lack of confidence in their feelings or trouble verbalizing their thoughts. Other people have trouble listening. Even when someone else is talking, they interrupt or are thinking about what they want to say next. For communication to work, there has to be a two way connection and both parties need to talk and listen.

When you think about it, so many problems in life come from a lack of good communication. In fact, most TV sitcoms are based on people misunderstanding each other or misunderstanding situations. As funny as those sitcoms can be, in real life, a lot of damage is done when feelings, information, and life events are not communicated properly. Families can be torn apart because we don't understand each other.

All of us need to work on the communication skill. Not only because it makes life better but because real communication can be very sacred. When someone shares intimately what is going on inside of them, it needs to be understood and treated with respect. Whether it is between nations, business people, spouses, siblings or friends, good communication makes the world much better.

PRAYER FOR THE BLESSING OF THE DAY...

Lord, help me listen today. Let me give others the opportunity to speak their hearts. And when it is my turn, let me share my life and my love, with Your words. AMEN.

Fr. Dale

February 3

ONE LESSON I HAVE LEARNED IN MY LIFE IS...

Life is a grindstone. It will either wear you down, or polish you to a shine.

PRAYER FOR THE BLESSING OF THE DAY...

Lord, please give me the gift of perspective. If things don't go as planned, help me go with how they have gone. If the carefully planned trip turns into a journey of twists and turns, remind me to look out the window and enjoy the ride.

Jody Serey

February 4

ONE LESSON I HAVE LEARNED IN MY LIFE IS...

We have to allow people to be human, and to be themselves. Sometimes, we put people (pastors, celebrities, sports figures, politicians) on a pedestal and then we are shocked when they can't live up to our expectations. All of us have strengths and weaknesses. All of us have good and bad seasons of life. We need to accept one another in the Spirit of Jesus.

Marilyn Monroe said something profound about this subject. She said, "I've never fooled anyone. I've let the people fool themselves. They didn't bother to find out who and what I was. Instead, they would invent a character for me."

My friends, we don't need any more characters in our world. We need real people who are doing the best they can with the gifts and talents God has given them.

PRAYER FOR THE BLESSING OF THE DAY...

Lord, help me not to prejudge anyone. Allow me to love and accept others with Your heart. AMEN.

Fr. Dale

February 5

ONE LESSON I HAVE LEARNED IN MY LIFE IS...

As I become more intimate with the Lord, I trust Him more and more with the trials of my life. I stand today – in faith – trusting in His sovereignty over me and praising His name even in the fire. Why? How? Because He has seen me through myriad ailments, disappointments, for a time, for a season. I am here looking back at those events, having survived...having been shaped by them into the person I am today. The Lord has carried me through some intense fires in my life. I trust Him to continue, because that is His character. Whatever lies ahead, I will trust Him always. He has shown me that He is trustworthy and He never changes. I WILL trust Him in the midst of any fire, over and over again.

TRUSTING JESUS

E.P. Stites (The Otterbein Hymnal – 1889)

Simply trusting ev'ry day,
Trusting thro' a stormy way;
Even when my faith is small,
Trusting Jesus, that is all.

21

Brightly doth His Spirit shine,
Into this poor heart of mine;
While He leads I cannot fall,
Trusting, Jesus, that is all.

Singing if my way is clear;
Praying if the path is drear;
If in danger for Him call;
Trusting Jesus, that is all.

Trusting as the moments fly,
Trusting as the days go by;
Trusting him whate'er befall,
Trusting Jesus, that is all.

Trusting him while life shall last,
Trusting him till earth is past;
Till within the jasper wall,
Trusting Jesus, that is all.

PRAYER FOR THE BLESSING OF THE DAY...

Thank you, my God for Your love, Your grace, Your protection, Your provision, Your peace. Thank you for never leaving me alone in my darkest hours. Thank you for lifting me up, out and beyond peace. Thank you for never leaving me alone in my darkest hours. Thank you for lifting me up, and beyond the trials. Thank you for ever drawing me to Your heart, for shaping me through the flames, into this person who kneels before You...broken and whole, emptied and renewed, lost and redeemed...trusting You, because You are my God.

Cheryl Armstrong

February 6

ONE LESSON I HAVE LEARNED IN MY LIFE IS...

Kindness matters. I know that is the title of a book that Jody Serey and

I have written. But it's more than a title -- it is TRUTH. It seems like our world has become less kind than ever before. Politicians call each other names. People who disagree tear each other down. In our work places, people are mean to each other. And, even in our churches, we say a lot more than our prayers.

In the book, Kindness Matters, I wrote the following: "Basic human decency and human kindness matter. The simple things our mothers taught us, and that we learned in kindergarten, are still true and valuable. 'Thank you', 'hello', 'I am sorry', 'Glad to see you' still carry tremendous weight even in our world filled with tweeting and texting." (page 55)

We sure can't control how others react; we can always choose to respond with Christian kindness.

PRAYER FOR THE BLESSING OF THE DAY...

Colossians 3:12

"Therefore, as God's chosen people, holy and beloved, clothe yourselves with compassion, kindness, humility, gentleness, and patience."

Fr. Dale

February 7

ONE LESSON I HAVE LEARNED IN MY LIFE IS...

God calls us to be a good influence in the lives of others. The word "influence" originally had to do with the alignment of the stars and the impact that alignment had on the character and the destiny of people. Now, we know that it isn't the stars that have strong impact on people, but rather the power people have in shaping the behavior of others. The bible is filled with quotes about helping others by giving good example. Proverbs 13:20 says "Become wise by walking with the wise; hang out with fools and watch your life fall to pieces."

The bible is also clear about the punishment for being a bad influence. Luke 17:2 says "It would be better for you if a millstone were hung around your neck and you were thrown into the sea than for you to cause one of these little ones to stumble."

It is true that we don't control the choices of others. But by word and

23

example, we can sure inspire others to make better choices.

PRAYER FOR THE BLESSING OF THE DAY...

Help me Lord to give good example today by loving You and others. AMEN.

Fr. Dale

February 8

ONE LESSON I HAVE LEARNED IN MY LIFE IS...

Sometimes I have to hear something more than once before I understand it. Let me explain. The other day I heard someone say, "We should forgive those who have not yet hurt us so that when they do hurt us, we don't have to worry about it." When I first heard these words, I thought to myself that doesn't make sense, how can I forgive someone for something that they haven't done? And, how can I forgive someone when I don't know how deep the hurt is? And the answer is: that is the whole point. What they were saying is "don't focus on the hurt, focus on the forgiveness." In other words, we should have such an attitude of forgiveness that the choice to forgive has already been made.

The more I thought about it, the more right it sounded. That is what Jesus did for us. Long before we were born, and long before we ever sinned, He forgave us. He did not focus on the wrongs we were going to do, rather He focused on US and our need for His mercy. If I want to be more like Jesus I need to choose to forgive... no matter who hurts me, when they hurt me, or how they hurt me. My focus needs to be on forgiveness.

PRAYER FOR THE BLESSING OF THE DAY...

Our Father, who art in heaven, hallowed be thy name.

Thy kingdom come, thy will be done, on earth as it is in heaven.

Give us this day our daily bread. And forgive us our trespasses, as

We forgive those who trespass against us. And lead us not into

Temptation, but deliver us from evil. AMEN.

Fr. Dale

February 9

ONE LESSON I HAVE LEARNED IN MY LIFE IS...

Grief is different for everybody who experiences a loss. There is no right or wrong way to grieve, and no two people react the same way to a broken heart. The widow who seems "fine" after a few months may be good at putting on a brace face, and the father who has buried a son may not be able to listen to the happy sounds of a football game for the rest of his life.

We must embrace each other when there are no words. We must comfort each other when pain seems all that is left. We stand between the bereft and the abyss. And at any time on any day, it may be our turn to need the feel of arms around us.

PRAYER FOR THE BLESSING OF THE DAY...

Lord, help me hear the silent cries in the night of the ones who fear You have abandoned them. Let me find ways to reassure, to help calm the terror of being alone, and to be the face of Christ amidst the chaos. And when I stand weeping in the night, please open my ears to the voices of the ones who would call me out of the darkness.

Jody Serey

February 10

ONE LESSON I HAVE LEARNED IN MY LIFE IS...

We all have problems. No one lives a perfect life. No one actually lives in Camelot. Life is what it is -- and it comes filled with both blessings and issues. Having said that, the truth is that life deals some people more problems than others. And, the truth also is that some folks by their choices create more problems for themselves (and others). The most important thing any of us can learn about the problems of life is that we have to deal with them. We cannot ignore them and think they will go away. The great thing about our faith is that we never have to face them alone. We face our issues, every day, with the power and the grace of God. The Gospel of Matthew tells us that worrying about a problem does nothing. It doesn't add a day to our lifetime nor does it add any quality to our life. Doing what we can, making good choices, praying to God for discernment, and relying upon God's grace seem to be the best path for facing the problems of life. We are so blessed to have a God who loves us and who walks with us as we journey through life.

PRAYER FOR THE BLESSING OF THE DAY...

Peter 5: 6-7

"Humble yourselves, therefore, under God's mighty hand, they He may lift you up in due time. Cast all your anxiety on Him because He cares for you."

Lord, I ask Your help as I face the blessings and the issues of my life. AMEN.

Fr. Dale

February 11

ONE LESSON I HAVE LEARNED IN MY LIFE IS...

Today is National Inventors' Day. While there have been many things invented over the centuries, one only needs to look around to see the most amazing creations of God.

We need to thank God for all of life's treasures and talents bestowed on us. We need to use them wisely and for His greater glory even in our own imperfect way.

PRAYER FOR THE BLESSING OF THE DAY...

Heavenly Father, I am so thankful for all Your blessings in my life. Help me to recognize the ways in which I can use them to serve You.

Peter Rehm

February 12

ONE LESSON I HAVE LEARNED IN MY LIFE IS...

Good friends are hard to come by. I have learned that there are people who are just acquaintances and there are people who are true friends.

People need more true friends in their lives to guide them through. While it is important to have a number of people you can get along with, like acquaintances, the qualities of a true friend are irreplaceable.

There are many differences between an acquaintance and a true friend. Acquaintances are the coworker or the guy you "make friends with" at the supermarket. But, real friends are the ones you can trust indefinitely. They are the people you can depend on to get you through. They are the people who you tell everything to, and love unconditionally. I feel that we need to show more love to that inner circle of real friends. And make sure that we stay in touch with them and see how they are doing. I have learned that even a simple "How are you?" can make a person's day. Let us make sure to reach out our love to those who need it.

PRAYER FOR THE BLESSING OF THE DAY...

God, thank you for bestowing on me the gift of wonderful people in my life. I am truly thankful for them, and for the fact that You put them into my life.

Let me remember to reach out with tenderness and love to those around me, and to connect with my true friends. AMEN.

Peter Rehm-Gerdes

February 13

ONE LESSON I HAVE LEARNED IN MY LIFE IS...

We need to appreciate the people God puts in our lives. Today is my dad's birthday. He passed away in 2003. Somehow we forget that our loved ones will not be here forever. My dad was a Marine and was sometimes pretty tough. My dad could also be extremely tender and generous. But one thing for sure my dad taught us was the importance of family. Memories of my dad will live on in me. I hope I am learning to be more appreciative of people every day.

PRAYER FOR THE BLESSING OF THE DAY...

Father, thank you for the many blessings You have given me. Especially, I thank You for the people who love me, and those that I love. Help me to show gratitude to You and to others.

Fr. Dale

February 14

ONE LESSON I HAVE LEARNED IN MY LIFE IS...

That love is not a feeling -- it is a decision! Feelings go up and down; today I feel close to someone, and tomorrow I feel distant. But that is not love. Real love is about commitment. I promise to love you, no matter what. I promise to put your needs on equal par with my own. When we love, we give ourselves to another, no matter what we feel.

Some principles are true with God. Loving God is not about a spiritual high; it's about a commitment to love Him and serve Him, no matter what! And by the way -- Happy Valentine's Day!

PRAYER FOR THE BLESSING OF THE DAY...

Lord, make me a more loving person. Help me to stop being so self-centered and so tied to my own emotions. Help me to commit my heart to You, to my family, to others.

And Lord, let me remember today the words of Mother Teresa, "Love begins by taking care of the closest ones – the ones at home."

Fr. Dale

February 15

ONE LESSON I HAVE LEARNED IN MY LIFE IS...

We all need to read the bible on a regular basis. The bible is God's word --that is, God's revelation to us. It is God telling us about Himself and revealing His way for us.

I opened the bible this morning. As I started to read the first letter of Timothy (5:11-12), the Lord said, "Pursue righteousness, godliness, faith, love, endurance and gentleness. Fight the good fight of faith; take hold of eternal life."

Wow. I don't think I can get any better encouragement or wisdom than that.

PRAYER FOR THE BLESSING OF THE DAY...

From the prophet Jeremiah (15:16-17)

"Your words were found, and I ate them; your words became a joy to me and the delight of my heart; for I am called by your name, O Lord, God of hosts."

Fr. Dale

February 16

ONE LESSON I HAVE LEARNED IN MY LIFE IS...

A Valentine from a small child should stay under the magnet on the refrigerator door for the rest of the year.

PRAYER FOR THE BLESSING OF THE DAY...

Lord, make my eyes fresh every time I look on the tokens of love offered me by the ones You have brought into my life. Let me honor every gesture, every gift with gratitude. Don't let me take for granted any one of them whose hearts carry me inside.

Jody Serey

February 17

ONE LESSON I HAVE LEARNED IN MY LIFE IS...

Forgiveness is one of life's best gifts. Whenever I was wronged, I used to want justice or retribution. This never left me feeling whole or happy. After many years of experiencing disappointment with partners, family, and life, I learned that I possessed the power to feel joy. All I had to do is forgive and life got better. It is still not easy but it comes more quickly. Forgiveness is grace I can enjoy whenever I choose it.

PRAYER FOR THE BLESSING OF THE DAY...

I pray for a tender heart that is always ready to accept and love just as my creator loves me. AMEN.

Brad Kuluris

February 18

ONE LESSON I HAVE LEARNED IN MY LIFE IS...

Job is a great role model. I hope I can always remain as faithful as he was. At the same time, I pray my life (and yours) never gets as bad as Job's.

Job was never some kind of super hero or saint. He was an ordinary man who was stripped naked of everything in this life. He lost his wealth, his children, his health, and his friends. But he never lost his faith in God.

For a time in my life, I felt like Job. Maybe you have felt that way as well. In the end, Job never cursed God. Job said (42:5) "I know You can do all things, and that no purpose of Yours could ever be thwarted."

PRAYER FOR THE BLESSING OF THE DAY…

Job said (Job 19:25-26)

"I know my redeemer lives and that at last, he will stand upon the earth; and after my skin has been thus destroyed, then in my flesh I shall see God."

Fr. Dale

February 19

ONE LESSON I HAVE LEARNED IN MY LIFE IS…

Life is not always what you expect. This is the day my best friend and sometimes my worst enemy for 50 years was born. We were friends for two and a half years, and then we married. The wars and power struggles between the two of us began. When we added children to this love/hate relationship, the battles increased and intensified. The intensity grew into threats that turned into requests for a divorce.

These battles were all related to our different interpretations of Ephesians 5:22-33: "Wives, submit to your own husbands…"

My husband's interpretation of this passage stopped after the word "husbands". My interpretation of this passage continued until the end of verse 33. "Wives, submit to your own husbands as to the Lord… For the husband is the head of the wife even as Christ is the head of the church his body, and is himself its Savior… Now as the church submits to Christ, so also wives should submit in everything to their husbands…"

It took me 10 years before I understood I needed to submit to God, and as I submitted to God I then in turn submitted to my husband. This simple understanding of God and my submission to Him began changing my heart and attitude. As God changed my heart and attitude, my husband's heart and attitude began to change.

No, life was not blissful ever after. But now we had a mutual understanding of who we were in God's eyes, and how God wanted us to relate to each other and to Him.

PRAYER FOR THE BLESSING OF THE DAY...

Lord, thank you for Words of wisdom. You made each of us. You brought each of us together. You have patiently taught us how to love You and submit to You and to each other. Lord, Your strength flows through Your love for us so we in turn can love and strengthen each other.

Carol Taylor

February 20

ONE LESSON I HAVE LEARNED IN MY LIFE IS...

Never wear a white shirt to a barbecue.

PRAYER FOR THE BLESSING OF THE DAY...

Lord, when I disregard the consequences of my actions and provoke a disaster, I call on You to forgive me, and I ask You to rescue me from the folly of my own hand. In You all things are made whole again.

Jody Serey

February 21

ONE LESSON I HAVE LEARNED IN MY LIFE IS...

To trust in God that He will help me through anything, if I ask him.

To believe that He wants me to feel safe in His hands, and that I am never alone to face my worries.

To love my life and to appreciate everything I have, and accept the good things and work on the bad things with Him at my side.

I picked this day because it is a special day God chose for my birthday.

PRAYER FOR THE BLESSING OF THE DAY...

My dearest God, You are my strength. My love for You keeps me on the right path for my journey toward heaven. Thank you for my precious life! AMEN.

Barbara Canchola

February 22

ONE LESSON I HAVE LEARNED IN MY LIFE IS...

I need God's presence every moment of every day. When I pray each morning, I give thanks for all God's Blessings and ask forgiveness for times I've disappointed Him. I pray for His presence in all my daily activities around the house and when I leave the confines of my "Comfort Zone" and venture outside. Never knowing what I might encounter, I try to face each challenge head on, without fear.

Simple short prayers continually throughout the day remind me of God's presence around me. I know God's will is done on His time, not mine.

PRAYER FOR THE BLESSING OF THE DAY...

Lord, Your humble servant thanks You for Your abundant blessings, love and inner peace.

Anonymous

February 23

ONE LESSON I HAVE LEARNED IN MY LIFE IS...

To appreciate those who are sacrificing for others. At church we welcomed a young woman and her three children. In the process of introducing herself and her little ones, she shared that her husband is in the military currently deployed in Iraq. As the worship continued, each of the children needed her attention and she provided it lovingly and quietly.

It reminded me of times when I experienced the same situations. My husband served in the Air Force for almost thirty years and often his assignments took him far away from us. The children and I either remained at our home base or moved nearer to my family. It was an incredible challenge for everyone.

I vividly remember one year when my husband was stationed overseas where Bob Hope brought his Christmas special to the troops. My husband was fortunate enough to see the show and wrote us all the details. When it was televised a few months later, our seven year old was convinced she would see her daddy among the thousand faces on the screen. She did not and sobbed for days.

So, the next time you see someone in uniform and thank them for their service, please do the same for their family who also sacrifice and serve.

PRAYER FOR THE BLESSING OF THE DAY...

Loving God, we thank You for the military who defend our country and for the families who love and support them. Please give each one the strength and courage needed to complete their mission. We offer this prayer in Your name. AMEN.

Scripture: Matthew 5:1-12

Betty Clewell

February 24

ONE LESSON I HAVE LEARNED IN MY LIFE IS...

All of us tend to be self-centered. In a real sense, it's a natural state of being for humans. From the time we are born, we are more aware of our own hungers and wants than we are of the needs of others. That's why many times, even when we appear to be helping someone else, we are really fulfilling our own need to be needed.

C.S. Lewis said, "The natural life in each of us is something self-centered, something that wants to be pitied and admired." But God offers us something more. He offers us a supernatural life. And on that level, we can learn to love, to give without repayment, to imitate God who always has the incredible ability to be other-centered.

PRAYER FOR THE BLESSING OF THE DAY...

Lord, teach me to be like You.
Let me love, without fear.
Let me be other-centered in my relationships.
Teach me how to care. AMEN.

Fr. Dale

February 25

ONE LESSON I HAVE LEARNED IN MY LIFE IS...

"Boredom" is no fun! For so many years of my life I was so busy I actually prayed for boredom...or at least to have nothing to do or think about. In 2005, when it happened to me, the boredom began to feel like a prison. Then I began to pray for the opportunity to do something that mattered. I am blessed that God gave me the chance to serve again.

Boredom, however, is more than having nothing to do. Boredom comes when we are un-engaged in what we are doing. I pray I can become more aware of God and the gift of life He has given me -- and that I can live my life fully ALIVE for God.

PRAYER FOR THE BLESSING OF THE DAY...

Wake up my spirit, Lord.

Let me see Your presence each day in my life. No matter what life brings, let me live my days fully alive in You.

AMEN.

Fr. Dale

February 26

ONE LESSON I HAVE LEARNED IN MY LIFE IS...

My view of what is sacred has changed. Like many people, I thought churches, rosaries, prayer books, and crosses were the things that were sacred. In my view now, people who love and places where God's love is made known are the real sacred things.

The word sacred means to make holy or to consecrate. For me, "holy" is where we encounter God. God is no more present in a prayer book than He is in the ocean. He is present everywhere. But, as humans, our deepest encounter with God will always be in LOVE. Dining tables, meals, picnics, laughter, compassion, are the sacred places. These are the places where love can be found and God can be met. In other words, sacred times and places can happen anywhere.

PRAYER FOR THE BLESSING OF THE DAY...

2 Chronicles 2:5-6

"The house that I am about to build will be great, for our God is greater than other gods. But who is able to build Him a house, since heaven, even highest heaven, can not contain Him."

Fr. Dale

February 27

ONE LESSON I HAVE LEARNED IN MY LIFE IS...

My life view for many years has been seeing the glass one-half empty and not one-half full. My negative outlook kept people away and I believe shut God out, also. God was trying to get my attention. However, because I saw so much of my world as negative, I didn't think God listened to me. When friends showed me how my negative energy kept them away, I saw how I also kept God distant. As I have changed to being a more positive human being, I have discovered that changing how I see things has had a profound effect on my relationship with God and those people (nearby) around me.

PRAYER FOR THE BLESSING OF THE DAY...

Thank you God for Your patience. Thank you God for loving me to this place of being more positive. I am so grateful for Your grace in helping me to grow in this area and of seeing Your love and caring in all I do. May I always see You, Lord, in my struggles of everyday life. Thank You for guiding me and for strengthening my beliefs.

Joal Fyten

February 28

ONE LESSON I HAVE LEARNED IN MY LIFE IS...

Silence often prevents an argument from beginning in the first place.

PRAYER FOR THE BLESSING OF THE DAY...

Lord, help me discern when the truth shall set me free, and when it is more important to be kind than to be right. It is often so hard to know when to speak up, and when to let a moment pass without my opinion being a part of it. If I cannot always be wise, please help me be merciful.

Jody Serey

February 29 (Leap Year)

ONE LESSON I HAVE LEARNED IN MY LIFE IS...

Born on February 29th? Do you still have a birthday? Does anyone wish you "Happy birthday?" Do you still age?

Of course the answer to all of these questions is yes -- you still have a birthday, you still celebrate, and you are still growing older.

Birthdays are important celebration days for the young and the old. It is the time to say "Hello, world here I am -- a wonderful creature created by God."

God celebrated my birthday even before He created the Universe.

[Ephesians 1:3-6 (The Message)] How blessed is God! And what a blessing He is! He's the Father of our Master, Jesus Christ, and takes us to the high places of blessing in Him. Long before He laid down earth's foundations, He had us in mind, had settled on us as the focus of his love, to be made whole and holy by his love. Long, long ago he decided to adopt us into His family through Jesus Christ. (What pleasure He took in planning this!) He wanted us to enter into the celebration of His lavish gift-giving by the hand of His beloved Son.

PRAYER FOR THE BLESSING OF THE DAY...

Thank you, Lord, for loving me and creating me even before You created Your expansive universe of which You made me part. Lord, as You created me, You birthed me, and You gave me a birthday to celebrate me as part of all Your creation. Thank you.

Carol Taylor

March 1

ONE LESSON I HAVE LEARNED IN MY LIFE IS...

Finding our true self, our true identity, is a lifelong project. We go through phases in our lives in which we identify ourselves by what we do, what we have, or how others perceive us. In time, we learn to go deeper and we begin to see ourselves as God sees us. We begin to see what God designed each of us uniquely and has given each of us different gifts and talents for us to use on our lives' journey.

One of my favorite Christian songs is by Casting Crowns and is called "Who Am I." The words ask the question "Who am I, that the Lord of all the earth would care to know my name, would care to feel my hurt? Who am I, I am a beloved child of God."

PRAYER FOR THE BLESSING OF THE DAY...

Ephesians 2:10

"For we are God's handiwork, created in Christ Jesus to do good works, which God prepared in advance for us to do."

Lord, allow me to become the person You created me to be. AMEN.

Fr. Dale

March 2

ONE LESSON I HAVE LEARNED IN MY LIFE IS...

That we are in the end times. What that means is that there are three periods of time: (1) before Christ; (2) of Christ; and (3) after Christ. None of us knows how long this third period will last -- it could end tonight or 10,000 years from now.

I recently heard an interview with someone who said I know we are close to the end times because the signs are clear. He went on to say that for him, the Kardashians being on TV must be an indication Jesus is coming soon. He was kidding, of course (I think!).

When we look around our world there are a lot of crazy things going on. Politics are a mess. Entertainers don't show talent anymore -- they show their foolishness. And, the economy continues to be out of whack. These are not signs of the end times. These are signs of how much we need God. We need to re-focus our agenda to move from a "self-centered" culture to a "life-giving" society that calls for dignity and respect for the world and each other.

PRAYER FOR THE BLESSING OF THE DAY...

Change me, Lord. Change our world. Let us seek to live a more digni-fied and respectful life. AMEN.

Fr. Dale

March 3

ONE LESSON I HAVE LEARNED IN MY LIFE IS...

God is not an enabler. He gives us the tools to live a good life and to get through hardships. His word, prayer, mentors, community, friends, family, and even events are tools. It's up to us to make the choice whether or not to learn to use these tools. He always answers prayers. Perhaps not in the way we expect ("no"), nor at the time we want ("not yet") -- but always in a way to help us grow, not just to fix it. What would we really learn that way? No, He is not an enabler. He loves us too much for that.

PRAYER FOR THE BLESSING OF THE DAY...

Lord, help me to be aware of Your lessons, to learn from them and always be open to daily miracles.

Elisa Trivanovich

March 4

ONE LESSON I HAVE LEARNED IN MY LIFE IS...

The words I speak make a profound impact on all those I encounter. Harsh words can seem just and fair at the moment, but these words cannot be erased as easily as they were spoken. Many harsh words spoken in anger can never be taken back. These unkind words stick like glue and sometimes, sadly, they can never be erased. They stay with people forever. Kind and loving words imprint on our soul and remain steadfast, bringing kindness, compassion and cherished memo-ries into someone's life. When speaking to a child, choose your words with a careful thought to lovingly last a lifetime. It is okay to hold your tongue and not speak at times if it will insult others.

Reflect on some of the kind words spoken to you in your life and how they remain with you. You can remember how old you were and the situation, down to what you ate that day. Those words possibly stayed with you if they were unkind and maybe remain with you today. There are so many opportunities in life to make a difference. Be a hero; create a memory by speaking kind words.

PRAYER FOR THE BLESSING OF THE DAY...

"Let no corrupting talk come out of your mouths, but only as is good for building up, as fits the occasion, that it may give grace to those who hear." Ephesians 4:29

Dear Lord, may I think before I speak and use my words to bring praise and comfort to others. Keep my heart open to allow my words to be loving. May I not speak any words with bitterness, hate or cursing and I implore You to be the author of my words.

You gave me a beautiful mind and the ability to speak. Let me honor You with my choices and start a revolution and be a "hero" of words. Let my words make a difference, show compassion and bestow powerful blessings to build others up and watch small miracles unfold.

Cindy A. Kiraly

March 5

ONE LESSON I HAVE LEARNED IN MY LIFE IS...

The more bitter the winter, the sweeter the spring.

PRAYER FOR THE BLESSING OF THE DAY...

Lord, help me be grateful for every day allotted me. Let me see the flowers that bloom, even if they open their faces on a battlefield. Strengthen my resolve to keep my heart open to the wonders of this earth, so that I don't become a stone that cannot rejoice.

Jody Serey

March 6

ONE LESSON I HAVE LEARNED IN MY LIFE IS...

I thought I knew love. Twenty seven years ago I made my vows to my love and God. I was naive to knowing love. I was blessed with a wonderful relationship. We had our days of trials during these years. We worked on our relationship daily and tried to put God first in our relationship. Each year as this day passes, I would realize that the day I first made those vows of love, I thought I knew love. The commitment of our relationship and our love for one another seemed to deepen more and more as the years went by. I was grateful for this love. Since our days are numbered here on earth, there came that day that the Lord called for my love to be with Him. The pain of not having my love beside me made me ache. I remain to have that ache and am willing to continue to have that ache. I call it my "love ache." But, from the lesson I've learned, I've been blessed to have been in a loving relationship that very few get to know. The outpouring of love given to me from family, friends, and church community is far more than I would ever imagine. Daily I continue to learn earthly love I obtain and am able to give, but what a greater love the Lord has for me.

PRAYER FOR THE BLESSING OF THE DAY...

Thank you for Your love, Lord.
Be devoted to one another in love.   *Romans 12:10*

I pray that you, being rooted and established in love, may have power, together with all the Lord's holy people, to grasp how wide and long and high and deep is the love of Christ. Ephesians 3:17,18

Kathy Davis (KD)

March 7

ONE LESSON I HAVE LEARNED IN MY LIFE IS...

It is best not to have one hero in your life, but rather have several role models that inspire you in areas of your life. I remember several years ago when NBA player Charles Barkley shocked everyone by saying "I am not a role model." It's true that he should not be the one we look at to see how to live. The problem is when we have one "hero," we are crushed if they fall. But, when we see characteristics and traits in others it is good to emulate those traits. Barkley is a good role model for hard work. Walt Disney can be a role model for creativity. Bill Gates may be a role model for generosity. When it comes to a hero -- or one person we look to as to how to live our lives -- that of course, should always be Jesus.

PRAYER FOR THE BLESSING OF THE DAY...

Lord Jesus, help me to be a better person. Help me to work hard, be kind, generous, and creative. But most of all, Jesus, help me to be more like You. AMEN.

Fr. Dale

March 8

ONE LESSON I HAVE LEARNED IN MY LIFE IS...

The greatest cure for anger is time.

PRAYER FOR THE BLESSING OF THE DAY...

Lord, help me get over it. Remind me to count to ten as many times as it takes to prevent actions I will regret, or to stop words that should not be said. Even when my anger is justified, be a calming voice that rises above whatever other voices may be raised.

Jody Serey

March 9

ONE LESSON I HAVE LEARNED IN MY LIFE IS...

Live each moment as if it were your last...

When I attended my first day in the seminary, there was an inscription over the doorway that read, "Live with death before your very eyes." At first I thought that this was not a very inviting welcome to those coming to learn to be ordained ministers of a church. I soon realized it was the very best thing that I could learn. That inscription is the first rule of The Order of St. Benedict. He wanted his order to know that the greatest way we could serve God, is by making sure we live each moment of our life to the fullest. To give our all no matter what the task is at hand.

I have learned over the years that so many live with the regrets of the should ofs, would ofs, or could ofs. Those missed opportunities of things that they have put off until it's too late. I have started to live my life in a different way, to live as if this was the last moment I was on the earth. I find myself saying "love you" more to the people that are near and dear. I don't hold onto anger, and find myself reconciling as quickly as I can. I never take a moment for granted with the people l meet.

As Christians, we need to understand that we have been blessed by God for everything going on in our lives. Let's not take one moment for granted. Let's live with death before our very eyes.

PRAYER FOR THE BLESSING OF THE DAY…

Scripture: Luke 12:20

Lord, give me the strength today to live my life to the fullest no matter what is asked of me, so that through my words, actions and deeds, I always give glory to Your name. AMEN.

Mark Dippre

March 10

ONE LESSON I HAVE LEARNED IN MY LIFE IS…

Don't give in to discouragement. We have all experienced discouragement at some time. It is part of life. But feeling it for a moment and giving in to it are two different things. Even the word should scare us. "Dis" means to get rid of…and courage comes from the Latin word cor which means heart. So to become discouraged means to get rid of "heart." It's not a good way to live.

I saw a quote recently from someone named Bob Moore. He said, "My strength did not come from lifting weights. My strength came from lifting myself up when I was knocked down."

Life can bring some hard knocks. Many times we may feel like we can't try again. But we can! Christ fell three times on his way to be crucified. But he got up and kept going. We may end up getting crucified just like Jesus, but in the meantime, our hearts need to stay strong! No discouragement!

PRAYER FOR THE BLESSING OF THE DAY…

Lord, let my eyes be focused on You. Keep my heart and spirit strong as I try to follow You with passion and love. AMEN.

Fr. Dale

March 11

ONE LESSON I HAVE LEARNED IN MY LIFE IS...

Nothing is a matter of life or death, except a matter of life or death.

PRAYER FOR THE BLESSING OF THE DAY...

Lord, grant me the gift of perspective. No object is more important than the person who dropped it and broke it. No amount of money is more valuable than the soul it might destroy. Remind me that if I have a piece of bread to eat with my water, and a seat in the shade, I am more fortunate than most people on the planet.

And if a material item becomes the focus of my attention and not my relationships with the ones I say I love – then help me turn my eyes towards You that I might again see what truly matters.

Jody Serey

March 12

ONE LESSON I HAVE LEARNED IN MY LIFE IS...

"People watching" is one of my favorite things to do. On a day off, it's great to get a cup of coffee and watch people at Starbucks or at the mall. What you learn is that each person is unique. And, that many people are kind of "weird." I know that it's not politically correct to say that, but it is true.

Yogi Berra once said, "You can observe a lot by watching." Mmmm, boy, is that true! What I've learned is this…that a lot of people don't treat each other very well. I've learned that lots of folks prefer drama over peace. I've learned that everybody has a different sense of taste, class, and different standards of conduct. And the other thing I've learned is that no one really cares what I think! And, that is very refreshing. My thoughts, judgments, and critical comments (in my head) don't mean anything. So, the best thing I can do is learn to accept people for who they are.

PRAYER FOR THE BLESSING OF THE DAY...

Father, help me to accept each person I meet today. And, help those I meet choose to accept me for who I am. AMEN.

Fr. Dale

March 13

ONE LESSON I HAVE LEARNED IN MY LIFE IS...

Surrendering is one of the hardest thing for any of us to do. I often say that 95 percent of us are control freaks and the other 5 percent are liars. We all want control. We all think we know what is best. But the spiritual life starts with surrender. When we say "God, You are in control" we become truly free to live and enjoy all that God has in store for us. God's will for us is our happiness and our fulfillment. He will always give us what is best for us. Turning control over to Him only makes life better. It is really worth letting go and letting GOD!

PRAYER FOR THE BLESSING OF THE DAY...

Heavenly Father, I surrender control of my life to You. I trust You. I believe in Your love for me. I am Yours.

Fr. Dale

March 14

ONE LESSON I HAVE LEARNED IN MY LIFE IS...

Karma is for real. I know that may sound odd coming from a Christian pastor. But it is true. What karma is, in Hindu and Buddhist beliefs, is that the sum of a person's actions in this life, affect what happens in the future. The reason I know it is true because St. Paul says the same thing, just in a different way. In his letter to the Galatians (6: 7), "A man reaps what he sows. Don't be misled -- you cannot mock the justice of God. You will always harvest what you plant. Do not be deceived. God is not mocked, for whatever one sows, that he will also reap." Seems pretty clear to me!

PRAYER FOR THE BLESSING OF THE DAY...

Prayer of St. Francis:

Lord, make me an instrument of Your peace.

Where there is hatred, let me sow love.

Where there is injury, pardon;

Where there is doubt, faith;

Where there is despair, hope;

Where there is darkness, light;

Where there is sadness, joy.

AMEN.

Fr. Dale

March 15

ONE LESSON I HAVE LEARNED IN MY LIFE IS...

That there are no guarantees in life; live it to the fullest. Thank God for everything you have, love truly and have faith in the Lord; because without faith you have nothing. A person without faith in the Lord is an empty vessel, so thank the Lord for all you have. Stop waiting for the storm to pass and learn to dance in the rain.

PRAYER FOR THE BLESSING OF THE DAY...

God, for another day, for another hour to live and serve You, I am truly grateful. Free me from fear of the future, from anxiety for the tomorrows; from bitterness toward anyone; from laziness in face of work; from failure before opportunity; from weakness when Your power is at hand. But fill me with love that knows no barrier; courage that cannot be shaken; faith strong enough for the darkness; strength sufficient for my task; loyalty to Your kingdom's goals. Be with me for another day and use me as You wish; in Your name I pray. AMEN.

(Proverbs 3:5-6)

Trust in the Lord with all your heart and lean not on your own understanding; in all your ways submit to Him, and He will make your paths straight.

Weldon L. Turner

March 16

ONE LESSON I HAVE LEARNED IN MY LIFE IS...

Make someone happy and you will be, too. I picked my birthday because that has always been a very special day in my life. I was raised in a big and loving family and I was blessed to have a wonderful childhood and lots of great friends. But I never shared a birthday with anyone till I met a great friend at Praise and Worship. Now it's even more special once a year to celebrate together.

PRAYER FOR THE BLESSING OF THE DAY...

Every day is God's gift to you. What you do with it is your gift to God.

Janet Eicher

March 17

ONE LESSON I HAVE LEARNED IN MY LIFE IS...

St. Patrick's Day isn't just for the Irish. In fact, St. Patrick belongs to us all. Most folks don't realize that St. Patrick was actually born in Roman Britain. None of that really matters, though. Patrick is an example of a man who became passionate about spreading Christianity. Patrick is credited with writing one of the most beautiful prayers ever (St. Patrick's Breastplate).

Christ with me,

Christ before me,

Christ behind me,

Christ in me,

Christ beneath me,

Christ above me,

Christ on my right,

Christ on my left,

Christ when I lie down,

Christ when I sit down,

Christ when I arise,

Christ in the heart of every man who thinks of me,

Christ in the mouth of everyone who speaks of me,

Christ in every eye that sees me,

Christ in every ear that hears me.

PRAYER FOR THE BLESSING OF THE DAY...

Lord, on this St. Patrick's Day, give me the desire to be immersed in the person of Jesus Christ. May my heart life be filled with Him. AMEN.

Fr. Dale

March 18

ONE LESSON I HAVE LEARNED IN MY LIFE IS...

Some words are unappealing. I don't like the word "petty." According to the dictionary, the word means trivial, minor, unimportant, insignificant, and inconsequential. To be honest, none of these words are appealing, either. Yet some people live their lives reacting to petty things. They put so much emphasis on things that really don't matter. If I am not careful, I can do that, too. I begin to worry, and then put time and energy into things that don't matter. The things that matter are the things of God's Kingdom, the things that make life better here on Earth, and the ways we love each other. I pray, hard, I never become a petty person.

PRAYER FOR THE BLESSING OF THE DAY...

Lord, give me the gift of discernment. Help me to know the difference between what matters to You and what is unimportant in building Your kingdom. AMEN.

Fr. Dale

March 19

ONE LESSON I HAVE LEARNED IN MY LIFE IS...

When you reach for the rose, you also grasp the thorn.

PRAYER FOR THE BLESSING OF THE DAY...

Lord, help me remember that nothing is as perfect as Your love. Behind great beauty can be a source of pain. The petals and perfume of the rose can be enjoyed without harm to their admirer if the rose is touched gently, and with respect. May I always handle my relationships with others with care.

Jody Serey

March 20

ONE LESSON I HAVE LEARNED IN MY LIFE IS...

When it comes to forgiveness, it's never about the other person; it is always about who I choose to be. There is no doubt that forgiveness is much easier when someone is sincerely sorry for the hurt they caused. But I need to forgive not because the other person is sorry, but because I choose to follow Christ. If I simply stay in my hurt and anger, I cannot get closer to Christ. As a disciple of Jesus, I must accept His heart and in doing so, find a way to turn everything over to Our Father. Once I let go, God can do with the other person whatever He chooses. I am free!

PRAYER FOR THE BLESSING OF THE DAY...

Dear Jesus,

You have taught us to love others as we love ourselves. Just as I desire forgiveness from You, I must be willing to forgive others. Your word teaches us, "the measure You use will be measured back to You" (Luke 6:38). May I give forgiveness generously. AMEN.

Fr. Dale

March 21

ONE LESSON I HAVE LEARNED IN MY LIFE IS...

People can change. Trust me when I say that people often don't change. Much of the time, that is the choice they make. Because of that, sayings like a "leopard doesn't change its spots" seem true. But with grace and good choices, change is possible. The whole gospel is based upon the hope of human change.

In the New Testament, we see many stories of change. Zacchaeus the tax collector turned from his "crooked" ways and returned money he gained unfairly. If he could change, anyone can.

The bottom line is we always have to give people every opportunity to right their wrongs. And, if they are trying, we do something "un-Godly" by holding them back. As long as we are alive, there is no limit to what God's grace can do.

This, my friends, is good news. And with good news we have hope that we too, can change.

PRAYER FOR THE BLESSING OF THE DAY...

Father, let me be more like Your son, Jesus. Let me give everyone in my life the opportunity and the encouragement to grow and be better. And thank you, Father, for continually showering Your grace on me so I too can change. AMEN.

Fr. Dale

March 22

ONE LESSON I HAVE LEARNED IN MY LIFE IS...

Not only have others hurt me, but I have hurt others. Whether I meant to hurt someone, or even knew I hurt them, there are many I have caused pain. My guess is, so have you. What do we need to do? First, we need to ask forgiveness if we are given the opportunity. Second, we must pray for the people we have hurt. And finally, we have to become more aware of how our actions impact others. Although I am not a parent, I think it is especially true that over a lifetime we can hurt those who we love most. God is always merciful. We hope those around us are, too.

PRAYER FOR THE BLESSING OF THE DAY...

Today, Lord, I pray for anyone I have hurt over my life time. I ask forgiveness of You, and them. Heal all who are hurting, Lord. And let Your love shine through the brokenness of us all. AMEN.

Fr. Dale

March 23

ONE LESSON I HAVE LEARNED IN MY LIFE IS...

You should never confuse the value of something with its cost. A diamond engagement ring becomes a bitter token after a divorce. But if you had to insure a three-year-old's handprint in plaster, you'd need to take out a million dollars in coverage.

PRAYER FOR THE BLESSING OF THE DAY...

Lord, thank You for the true treasures of my life -- the gold of a sunset, the silver of moonlight, the diamond glitter of the stars. Let me fill up with gratitude even when my pockets are empty, and remind me over and over again that if my eyes saw daylight this morning, and my ears heard the birds – my day was rich beyond measure.

Jody Serey

March 24

ONE LESSON I HAVE LEARNED IN MY LIFE IS...

I cannot second guess God. March 24, 1968 I had just arrived in Vietnam 24 hours earlier. I was assigned to a medical unit in the Central Highlands. The next day I was assigned to go out on an ambush patrol with a platoon of soldiers. Our mission was to stop the rocket attacks on our base camp. While we were almost to the point of setting up our ambush, the South Vietnamese soldiers started shooting at us. I got pushed down by a guy named Benny Dale Cash. In his doing so, he took a round to his left side. My bullet. I crawled over to him and turned on his and my flashlight so I could see his wound. Big mistake. Now I was sitting up over him bandaging his wound and giving him a shot of morphine. I was outlined by the light and I felt bullets pass right by me. Finally the shooting stopped and we got Benny Cash back to the base camp, and he went into surgery. I visited him a few times in the hospital, as I was very thankful for him pushing me down. 28 days later he died due to liver failure. His death has always bothered me. Why him, and not me?

I would always wonder why God spared my life, and the only thing I can figure out is He was not done with me yet. He allowed me to

50

become someone's husband, someone's father, someone's grandfather. He gave me three great careers. I was in Vietnam at age 21 and I am 67 years old now. As I ask God why Benny and not me, and He has not answered the question. I have learned not to ask so many questions. I just know that I have been very blessed and will continue to be blessed as the years just continue on. I can only guess that God still has much more in store for me.

For someone who did not think he would live to be 22, I am amazed by God's love and kindness. Thanks, God. And bless Benny Cash.

PRAYER FOR THE BLESSING OF THE DAY...

Dear Lord, thank You for Your blessings and the gift of life. Please allow me to recognize the gifts You give to me as my family and friends. Allow me to be a blessing to others that I come in contact with. AMEN.

Kerry Pardue

March 25

ONE LESSON I HAVE LEARNED IN MY LIFE IS...

The number of atheists in the world continue to grow. The statistics don't lie, and for me as a Christian, it is a cause of great concern. But, the other lesson I have learned, is that many atheists don't reject God -- they reject the God that has been presented to them.

I recently asked a young man in counseling where he was with God. He answered, "You mean the psychotic angry old dude who takes revenge on anybody who doesn't do exactly what he says?"

I calmly replied, "No, the amazing Creator who unconditionally loves you and cries for you to spend eternity with Him." The young man was stunned.

God is not what was taught to us as little kids. God is not what we felt was crammed down our throats. God is bigger and more loving than any of that.

And as far as combating atheism, the best thing we can do is to present God in a much more loving way.

PRAYER FOR THE BLESSING OF THE DAY...

Lord, I pray for all those who do not believe in You. I ask forgiveness for times I have misrepresented You. You are a loving and amazing God. AMEN.

Fr. Dale

March 26

ONE LESSON I HAVE LEARNED IN MY LIFE IS...

Age is no guarantee of maturity.

PRAYER FOR THE BLESSING OF THE DAY...

Lord, if I grow old, let me do it with wisdom and a sense of humor. Bring me to the fullness of years with the qualities of tolerance and compassion left intact. Help me refrain from pettiness, mean-spiritedness, and a sense of entitlement.

Jody Serey

March 27

ONE LESSON I HAVE LEARNED IN MY LIFE IS...

Thunderstorms are awesome. Now, I know that loud thunder is scary. And, I also know the lightning can cause damage, and rain is treacherous to drive in. But, what's better than going outside when the storm passes? The air is fresh, the rain starts to turn things green, and life seems to have some kind of new beginning.

The same is true with the thunderstorms of life. They can be loud, scary, and treacherous. But when the storm passes, there is new life and new possibilities in life.

I have been through thunderstorms. I was scared. But, new life followed. I hope the same is true for you.

Thunderstorms are rarely convenient. They don't ever happen on our schedule. But, sometimes it is the way that God uses to sweep out the old air and to make life fresh again.

PRAYER FOR THE BLESSING OF THE DAY...

Jesus, be with me in the storms of life just like You were in the boat with the apostles. Help me to survive the thunderstorms and make it through to the freshness on the other side. AMEN.

Fr. Dale

March 28

ONE LESSON I HAVE LEARNED IN MY LIFE IS...

God expects great things from us...

I don't remember much of the day that l was baptized. In fact, my parents said that l slept all the way through it. I do know that now I am a parent and have my own children baptized, I hear great things are commissioned for us to live. Every Christian around the world is commissioned with three special tasks.

One is to be priestly. To not live our lives any more by the ways of the world, but to walk instead in the footsteps of God. Second, we are called to proclaim that He is coming again in glory. As prophets, we are called to proclaim the good news. We must do so, not only with words, but our very actions as well. Third is the greatest gift of all. We are anointed as KING. We are heirs to the throne of the Kingship of God. That, my friends, is truly amazing.

Today, let us remember that the greatest gift that we have received is that of our baptism into the Christian way of life. May we live today as true disciples of His great Love.

PRAYER FOR THE BLESSING OF THE DAY...

Scripture: Mathew 3:17

Lord, You have called me to serve You in my words, actions and deed. Today, may l live the gift of faith You have given me in baptism. May all of my actions give glory to You. AMEN.

Mark Dippre

March 29

ONE LESSON I HAVE LEARNED IN MY LIFE IS...

We all need to do more good works. Now, before you freak out, let me say that no amount of good works can ever earn us salvation. Salvation is a gift. And, no amount of good works can ever make up for our sins. So, the reason to do good works has nothing to do with trying to impress God or earn our way to heaven. Then why more good works? Two reasons: (1) the world needs them, and (2) as people of faith, we want to share our faith with others.

The world needs more goodness. We need more kindness, more acts of compassion, and more generosity. Neighbors need more meals when they are sick, more cookies when they are new in the neighborhood, and more watching for the safety of each other.

And, you and I need to remember that we are the hands and feet of Jesus in the world today. Maybe through us, others can come to know the love of God.

PRAYER FOR THE BLESSING OF THE DAY...

Lord, help me to do good for Your kingdom. Give me a chance today, Lord, to do something good for someone else. May I be Your love for someone else today. AMEN.

Fr. Dale

March 30

ONE LESSON I HAVE LEARNED IN MY LIFE IS...

Everything in our life is subject to change. No matter what the situation is today, it will change, sooner or later, for better or for worse. Change is all around us; in nature, personal and work relationships, health and in our beliefs. What's going on certainly will not be the same for us tomorrow as it is today.

The one thing that will never change is God's love for us.

"Though our feelings come and go, His love for us does not. It is not wearied by our sins, or our indifference; and, therefore, it is quite relentless in its determination that we shall be cured of those sins, at

54

whatever cost to us, at whatever cost to Him." -C.S. Lewis

PRAYER FOR THE BLESSING OF THE DAY...

Psalm 136:26

"Give thanks to the God of Heaven, for his steadfast love endures forever!"

Ned Trivanovich

March 31

ONE LESSON I HAVE LEARNED IN MY LIFE IS...

Value the people you love. Life takes sudden changes. People get ill. They sometimes have something happen in their lives that overwhelms them. Sometimes life has a speed bump that seems too high for them to pass. We simply never know what is coming next. That is why we have to say "I LOVE YOU" more often. That is why we have to keep telling people we cherish them and believe in them.

I recently went through a situation which I thought I lost someone very close to me. My life would never have been the same without them. But, I had peace no matter what, that this person knew of my deep love for them. There are others, however, to whom I'm not as good at saying those words. I need to love more openly. I need to have so much love coming from me that other people see it...know it...and can depend on it!

PRAYER FOR THE BLESSING OF THE DAY...

Jesus, thank you for putting so much love in my heart for so many others. Please Jesus, never let me hide that love. Let me say "I love you" many times today. I love You, Jesus. AMEN.

Fr. Dale

April 1

ONE LESSON I HAVE LEARNED IN MY LIFE IS...

God has a great sense of humor.

April first has always been a day filled with practical jokes. It is a day that someone will try to pull something over on you just to hear those words being shouted out, "April Fools!"

As a child I loved this day to bring laughter and joy to my life. Now that I am older, I have to say that this day is a little more difficult for me to handle. As we get older life is filled with a lot more challenges. We have to look at all the tasks at hand and often many times we feel overwhelmed by the struggles that are brought our way. We may even wonder if God does have a sense humor by giving us so much to handle at once.

I have come to learn when we go through times of struggle, we need to step back and just have a good laugh. We need to remember the joy in our lives and see the happiness that is always there. God has filled each and every one of us with so much joy and love. He has called us to be childlike and to laugh. Today, may we remember the joy as a child and find our sense of humor and laughter with God and one another. Let's go out of our way to pull a prank to remind others not to take life too seriously, but instead to remember the joy and laughter God put into our hearts.

PRAYER FOR THE BLESSING OF THE DAY...

God, today may I remember the joy and love You have brought into my life. May I have the courage and strength to remind others to laugh with God. AMEN.

Scripture: Mark 10: 13-16 "Let the children come unto me."

Mark Dippre

April 2

ONE LESSON I HAVE LEARNED IN MY LIFE IS...

The seed for even the most beautiful flower starts out as a little dead thing. For it to bloom, it takes water, dirt, and patience on the part of the one who planted it.

PRAYER FOR THE BLESSING OF THE DAY...

Lord, please have patience with me on the days that my heart lies shriveled beneath my ribs. Call me out to love something even smaller than the size of my own soul when I can't look up to see the sky. Make me useful when I am the least worthy, when I have the least worth. Help me bloom, no matter where I stretch up to see Your light.

Jody Serey

April 3

ONE LESSON I HAVE LEARNED IN MY LIFE IS...

Find something in each day that is special; something that makes me smile or maybe a bit melancholy (thoughtful) -- something that reminds me to thank God for the gifts He has given me.

PRAYER FOR THE BLESSING OF THE DAY...

Dear Jesus, thank you for family, for friends and for the special blessings You have given me. Please continue to watch over me and guide me in all I do. AMEN.

Barbara Bovy

April 4

ONE LESSON I HAVE LEARNED IN MY LIFE IS...

I do not always get what I pray for. I guess there are a lot of reasons for that being true. First, I don't always pray for the right thing. Second, I don't always see what the best thing is for me or others. But, when my prayer is answered, I need to learn how to be more grateful. It's funny how intent I can be when I want something. And, after the prayer is fulfilled, I seem to get easily distracted.

God is not a vending machine. And prayer is not the four quarters we put in for a diet Coke. If the vending machine doesn't produce a soft drink we feel cheated. Some of us treat prayer the same way. But with God, everything we receive is a gift. God doesn't owe us anything.

So, I need to remember to say thank you to the God of all creation, who owes me nothing, but cares for me deeply.

PRAYER FOR THE BLESSING OF THE DAY...

God, for all the times I have failed to say THANK YOU, please accept my gratitude now. I am blessed to call You my Father. AMEN.

Fr. Dale

April 5

ONE LESSON I HAVE LEARNED IN MY LIFE IS...

Trials are, sometimes, just blessings in disguise. The blessings usually aren't obvious at the time, but when I look back at different scenarios in my life, I can see how God's plans for me have unfolded. An injury forced me to consider retiring earlier than I had planned. I prayed for guidance and direction because I was concerned about being able to meet my financial obligations on a reduced income, but when a part-time job opened up at the time I was discerning what path to take, I knew this was the answer to my prayers. Everything just fell into place.

Another incident was when I was laid up for a couple of months with a broken foot and was not permitted to go to work. This turned out to be a blessing in disguise because I had just recently taken on the duties as executor to my aunt's estate, which was overwhelming to me. I knew it was going to take a lot of time -- and now I had that time. God provided a way. Sometimes the blessing isn't so obvious until days, weeks, months, or even years later, but I've found that He answers my prayers. Waiting for the answers and trusting in God's plan is not an easy thing to do at times, even though, deep down in my heart, I know that He knows what is best for me.

PRAYER FOR THE BLESSING OF THE DAY...

Lord, I thank you for the many blessings that You have given me, including those that I didn't recognize at the time. Each time I reflect on difficult times in my life, I see Your presence and Your plans as they unfolded. Thank you for always being there for me, and helping me over each hurdle that I encounter. You are my Rock and my salvation. Lord, I ask You to strengthen my faith in You. Help me trust in Your will and to be ever mindful of all the blessings that I've received from You, especially those that I call family and friends. Please bless them, Lord. Please also bless Fr. Dale and Fr. Mark and the work that they do for all of us at the Praise and Worship Center. I ask these things in Jesus' name. AMEN.

M.J. Broudy

April 6

ONE LESSON I HAVE LEARNED IN MY LIFE IS...

The beach is a very spiritual place. I know many unspiritual things happen there. I know that beaches can be crowded and filled with dead fish and litter. But, when you stand at the edge of the water and look out -- it is amazing. The ocean is so vast and overwhelming, it is hard not to think of a magnificent creator who made it. And, when you add in a sunset, it is an incredible experience of God.

It's hard to have time to get to the beach. But we don't have to be there to be overwhelmed by God's glory. We can be in a crowd of people and see the vastness of God. Look outside your front door some evening and see the sunset right in front of your house. And if nothing else works, look at a picture of the Grand Canyon and remember who made it.

We have a God who is a masterful creator. What he has made, the oceans, the mountains, and the amazing stars, don't even begin to reflect His power.

PRAYER FOR THE BLESSING OF THE DAY...

Psalm 65

"The ends of the earth stand in awe at the sight to Your wonders.

The land of sunrise and sunset You fill with Your joy."

Thank you, Lord, for sharing Your beautiful creation with us. May I always be overwhelmed with Your love and power. AMEN.

Fr. Dale

April 7

ONE LESSON I HAVE LEARNED IN MY LIFE IS...

There is nothing free about freedom of speech, freedom of expression, freedom of religion, or freedom of choice.

Everything has a cost that is either direct or indirect. Freedom of anything comes with an enormous set of responsibilities.

PRAYER FOR THE BLESSING OF THE DAY...

Lord, let me always be aware of how my actions impact the feelings and well-being of others. Stay my hand from unintended violence and harm. Keep me ever mindful of the ripples that travel out from every stone I drop in still waters.

Jody Serey

April 8

ONE LESSON I HAVE LEARNED IN MY LIFE IS...

Our weaknesses are often our greatest gifts. Whatever has brought us to our knees, is what God will use to make us a help and comfort to others in a similar situation. If we allow ourselves to be vulnerable before strangers, "to tell our story" of addiction, illness, tragedy, wrong choices, etc., God can use us to help others. We can in some small way lead others to faith in Jesus if we allow God's will to be done in our lives.

This may sound illogical, but thank God for our weaknesses! Awareness of our weaknesses makes us know how dependent we are on God and helps us know Him more fully. In my weakest moments I can do nothing but cling to Jesus. I rejoice that I know him, am loved by Him in the middle of suffering.

PRAYER FOR THE BLESSING OF THE DAY...

2 Corinthians 4:7-9

7But we have this treasure in jars of clay, to show that the surpassing power belongs to God and not to us.

8We are afflicted in every way, but not crushed; perplexed, but not driven to despair;

9persecuted, but not forsaken; struck down, but not destroyed;

Suzanne Cline

April 9

ONE LESSON I HAVE LEARNED IN MY LIFE IS...

The living of life begins right now. For too long, I lived in the past and dreamed of the future while missing the majesty and beauty of the present. All of the things that I have regretted, I have never been able to change. All of the things that I have worried about never happened. What I missed, was the glory of God's presence in those moments and the gifts that He had for me then. It is in the present that we find God's greatest gifts.

Isaiah 54:7 "...with deep compassion, I will bring you back."

PRAYER FOR THE BLESSING OF THE DAY...

Please Lord, don't let me miss the glory of this day and this moment. Focus my mind on Your presence in the here and now. AMEN.

James M. Pelfrey

April 10

ONE LESSON I HAVE LEARNED IN MY LIFE IS...

"The end is sometime!" I recently saw a cartoon with a guy carrying a picket sign with that message on it. At first it struck me funny because I expected the sign to say "the end is near."But, who knows if that is true? "The end is sometime" is very profound.

Everything has an end. Your job will end. Your life will end. The world will end. And if we keep that in mind it helps us to enjoy the moment. Some people think talking about "the end" is depressing or scary. I don't think so. It is simply acknowledging the reality that this life, good and bad, is temporary. We need to enjoy it, embrace it, and cherish it. But we also need to know the limits of being human and being part of creation.

As far as the world coming to an end -- I promise you I don't have a clue how close it is. But I can promise you, "the end is sometime."So make each day MATTER.

PRAYER FOR THE BLESSING OF THE DAY...

Lord, thank you for today. Let me use this day to love, to believe, and to serve. And when the end comes, let me have no regrets. AMEN.

Fr. Dale

April 11

ONE LESSON I HAVE LEARNED IN MY LIFE IS...

Life isn't meant to be easy. It's meant to be lived. Sometimes happy, sometimes rough -- but with every up and down, you learn lessons that make you strong. Don't believe those who tell you they love you; believe those that show you they do. You have to embrace getting older, life is precious and when you've lost a lot of family and friends, you realize that each day is a gift. All things in life are temporary. If life is going well, enjoy it. It will not last forever. If life is going wrong, it won't last forever.

PRAYER FOR THE BLESSING OF THE DAY...

Faith is to believe what we do not see, and the reward of this faith is to see what we believe. (St. Augustine)

Janet Eicher

April 12

ONE LESSON I HAVE LEARNED IN MY LIFE IS...

Victor Hugo said, "To love another person is to see the face of God."

So whose face do we see when we allow ourselves to hate?

PRAYER FOR THE BLESSING OF THE DAY...

Lord, if the God in me can recognize the God in the person before me, we will both be saved from whatever destruction me might otherwise visit on each other. Violence of thought is truly real violence. Make me an instrument of Your peace. AMEN.

Jody Serey

April 13

ONE LESSON I HAVE LEARNED IN MY LIFE IS...

Time spent with friends and loved ones is time gained forever in memories.

PRAYER FOR THE BLESSING OF THE DAY...

Lord, let me never use the excuse "I'm too busy" when it comes to the people I love, and who love me. Press me forward into my clothes and into my car if there is a piano recital, a birthday party, a celebration, a peewee football game, a memorial. Let my face be the one that is looked for in the crowd, or in the pew. In good times and in bad, remind me what is truly worthy of my time and energy.

Jody Serey

April 14

ONE LESSON I HAVE LEARNED IN MY LIFE IS...

Is that we all want respect. No one likes being "dissed" -- that is, disrespected. When we stand in line, we want respect to be given to our turn. When someone greets us, we want to be treated like we matter. We don't want to be belittled.

I find it interesting that the term "dissed" is also used by techie people meaning to disconnect someone from the internet, server, or phone. Disconnecting someone can sure be a sign of no respect. It's like unfriending someone on Facebook.

Jesus respected all people, even sinners. We need to do the same. Treating someone like they are unwanted, unloved, or unimportant it's wrong. "Dissing" someone may make someone feel better than the other person, but at the same time we do it to someone else we are dissing their creator. Scripture says (1Peter 2:17) "Show proper respect to everyone, love the family of believers, fear God, honor the King." GREAT advice!

PRAYER FOR THE BLESSING OF THE DAY...

Dear God, teach me to respect myself, others, and You. Teach me how to treat others as You want me to treat them. AMEN.

Fr. Dale

April 15

ONE LESSON I HAVE LEARNED IN MY LIFE IS...

St. Paul is one of the most fascinating people of all time. What do we know of Paul? We know he was originally named Saul of Tarsus. He was born around 5 B.C. and died in 67 A.D. He is considered to be the father of modern Christianity. Paul studied to be a rabbi in the Pharisee party. While he was persecuting Christians, he had a conversion to Christ on the road to Damascus. He probably never met the person of Jesus until after the Resurrection and Christ appeared to him. And yet he founded churches, wrote thirteen letters in the New Testament, spent time in prison, survived a ship wreck on the island of Malta, and eventually died in the city of Rome.

Paul was a pastor. He taught about the cross and taught us all that we are free from the law as long as we live in Christ.

Every day we can open a bible and meet Paul. God has preserved his teachings for us. It's time we all become better friends with him.

PRAYER FOR THE BLESSING OF THE DAY...

Saint Paul says (Romans 13:8) "Owe no one anything, except to love one another for the one who loves another has fulfilled the law." AMEN.

Fr. Dale

April 16

ONE LESSON I HAVE LEARNED IN MY LIFE IS...

Life is filled with interruptions. If you are like me, you don't like most of them. Once in a while someone stops by with Starbucks and I can say I enjoy the interruption. But most days, I have a calendar, a list of priorities, and an agenda to get done. Any time someone tosses something in the middle of it, I am somehow thrown off.

C.S. Lewis has a different take on interruptions. He says, "Stop regarding all the unpleasant things as interruptions of one's 'real' life. The truth is of course that what one calls the interruptions are precisely one's real life -- the life God is sending day by day."

Lewis certainly puts a different spin on our agendas. Interruptions may be God's way to allow His agenda to impact our day. Given the two options, my agenda or God's, there is no doubt that His is far more important than mine.

PRAYER FOR THE BLESSING OF THE DAY...

Lord, let this day be filled with Your interruptions. Help me to rejoice in Your presence today.

AMEN.

Fr. Dale

April 17

ONE LESSON I HAVE LEARNED IN MY LIFE IS...

The three saddest words in the English language are, "I should have."

PRAYER FOR THE BLESSING OF THE DAY...

Guilt and regret are the tormenters of the grief-stricken. Lord, let me never waste another chance to speak a kind word, hold out a hand, or step off a familiar path to follow one who has wandered away into the weeds. Help me face the inevitable goodbyes in life with a peaceful heart knowing that what I could do, was done; what I could say, was said; and what love was needed, I offered up.

Jody Serey

April 18

ONE LESSON I HAVE LEARNED IN MY LIFE IS...

To keep a great relationship, one must not allow anger to control him/ her. Resentment may build as "a slow simmering pot" into bitterness. We must be honest with one another. The offense needs to be addressed quickly so the offense doesn't take hold and build. The anger must be resolved before one goes to bed. I have stayed up many a night into wee hours of the night physically tired, but I had made the promise to not allow the anger to fill my heart and let Satan have his way.

PRAYER FOR THE BLESSING OF THE DAY...

God, change my heart so I am not acting on my own selfish desires. I ask You to give me the wisdom and patience to turn my angered spirit to a loving spirit.

(Ephesians 4:26) "In your anger do not sin. Do not let the sun go down while you are still angry and do not give the devil a foothold."

(James 1:19-20) "My brothers, take note of this: Everyone should be quick to listen, slow to speak, and slow to anger because human anger does not produce the righteousness that God desires."

(Proverbs 19:11) "A hot-tempered person stirs conflict, but the one who is patient calms a quarrel. A person's wisdom yields patience; it is to one's glory to overlook an offense."

Kathy Davis (KD)

April 19

ONE LESSON I HAVE LEARNED IN MY LIFE IS...

Kindness and patience work better than anger. I have learned to take a deep breath, call on Jesus' name, and go forward from there.

PRAYER FOR THE BLESSING OF THE DAY...

Jesus, come to me. Be with me through hard times and good times. AMEN.

Jerry Bovy

April 20

ONE LESSON I HAVE LEARNED IN MY LIFE IS...

I want to live an authentic Christian life. On my good days, I know what that is. On other days, I seem to lose track. I guess to understand the authentic Christian life I need to take each word seriously. First, I need to be authentic and real. I can't pretend to be something or someone that I am not. Second, I need to imitate Christ and do all I can to put Jesus first in my daily life. To be a Christian means to see the world as Christ sees it, and to see others as Christ sees them. My daily choices need to reflect my Christian values. And third, in order to have a Christian life, I need to be alive. I need to feel, laugh, cry, enjoy, and cherish each moment as God's gift to me. Now that I see what the authentic Christian life is in writing I realize I understand what it is -- but that I have a long way to go to actually be living it. With God's grace, I believe I will get there one day!

PRAYER FOR THE BLESSING OF THE DAY...

Lord, may today be my day! May today be the day I truly follow You, trust You, and love You. Bless this day, Lord, and make it beautiful in Your sight. AMEN.

Fr. Dale

April 21

ONE LESSON I HAVE LEARNED IN MY LIFE IS...

The perfume of a delicate rose will fade, but the stink of the potato that got forgotten and rotted in the bin will still be there in six months.

PRAYER FOR THE BLESSING OF THE DAY...

Lord, if cleanliness is next to godliness, then our household may often seem unholy. Please accept the noise and disarray as offerings of life being lived and love being shared. Let our laughter be the hymns we lift up to You. And even if the banquet is less than elegant, we say to You that our table is surrounded by the ones who are grateful to the founder of all feasting.

Jody Serey

April 22

ONE LESSON I HAVE LEARNED IN MY LIFE IS...

We need to be a source of blessings for others. When we bless some-one, we are projecting goodness, kindness, and grace into their life. And when we bless, it is not simply saying words, but following those words up with actions. We do our best to bring life and goodness to someone else.

It's easy for all of us to get caught up in ourselves. But, with family, friends, and even strangers, we can become a source of something positive and Godly.

PRAYER FOR THE BLESSING OF THE DAY...

Prayer for others...traditional Irish blessing

"May the road rise up to meet you,
May the wind be always at your back,
May the sun shine warm your face,
The rains fall soft upon your fields,
And until we meet again,
May God hold you in the palm of his hand."
AMEN.
 Fr. Dale

April 23

ONE LESSON I HAVE LEARNED IN MY LIFE IS...

The human body is a magnificent work of God. And, God created the body to eventually break down and stop working. It is called AGING. Even though we should always do our best to care for our bodies (nutrition, exercise, etc.), we should not be surprised that our bodies are not eternal. AGING is not for wimps. It is not easy. But it is a way that God prepares us to let go of everything in this world. Our souls do not break down. They are eternal. The lesson is, we need to care for our souls. Our bodies get left behind; our souls live on forever.

PRAYER FOR THE BLESSING OF THE DAY...

Father, help me to be a good steward of both my body and my soul. Help me to recognize all things are a gift from You...and should be cherished by us.

 Fr. Dale

April 24

ONE LESSON I HAVE LEARNED IN MY LIFE IS...

The lens through which I look determines the vision I see. Everything is more than it appears. When viewed through the eyes of LOVE all is perfect and precious just as it is. Whether gazing at the brilliance of a starlit night or the tiny bubbles of a bubbling brook — or the myriad events that seem senseless, horrible and seeped in suffering and tragedy — all is invitation to peer deeper into the widening rings of the Divine Dance.

Clarity comes in glimpses and often right under my nose. It comes in the young homeless woman with hands and arms raised in prayer, or in the peaceful acceptance of a woman betrayed by her husband's extra-marital sex addiction who shares her journey from heartbreak through surrender to forgiveness.

Not long ago I spent an entire day sitting on the ground beside a rushing stream deep in the forest. There I became awakened to the lushness of the flowers and ferns, plants and towering trees flourishing alongside the fallen leaves and dead trunks and branches --- knowing then the truth of the unity of death and life.

There is a Glorious Presence manifested everywhere -- the All in All. If only we open our eyes and see.

PRAYER FOR THE BLESSING OF THE DAY...

My Lord and my God – as I wander through these days, may I see as You see – deeply through the eyes of LOVE. Show me the path You are laying out for me. Empower me to take steps along Your Way – with consciousness, compassion and courage. If the way becomes cloudy and difficult , help me to trust - keeping my eyes ever upon You.

Psalms 119:18, "Be generous with me and I will live a full life, not for a minute will I take my eyes off Your road. Open my eyes so I can see what You show me of Your miracle-wonders."

Anonymous

April 25

ONE LESSON I HAVE LEARNED IN MY LIFE IS...

Patience is a valuable virtue. When people get angry for no reason, or are fighting with someone else, it stems from a lack of patience.

If we all practiced patience, then there would be not as many conflicts, at home or national. With the "time is money" mantra of today's society, people seem to forget that there is time to spare. There is time to hear people out. There is time to talk things out with people.

If we look at the story of Job in the bible, he is a man of patience. In the beginning of the story, to prove Job's faithfulness to the Lord, God allowed the devil to destroy everything Job owned (Job 1). But Job knew that sometimes bad things happen to good people. He had patience and let God in to his life. He had faith that this was all part of God's plan. In the end God restored to Job twice as much as he had in the beginning (Job 42:10).

We need to have patience in today's world for the people around us, for the situations that happen to us, and for God's plan to play out in our lives.

PRAYER FOR THE BLESSING OF THE DAY...

Lord, grant me the gift of patience. Help me have the patience to function in the world around me. Give the gift of patience to everyone I see today, and enlighten them with Your grace, mercy, and unending love. AMEN.

Peter Rehm-Gerdes

April 26

ONE LESSON I HAVE LEARNED IN MY LIFE IS...

Forgiveness is an ongoing process for the forgiver. If you keep going back to a memory to see if it still hurts – it will. To truly let loose of the hurt over a wrongdoing, you have to leave the past in the past. There can be no moving forward if you keep looking back.

PRAYER FOR THE BLESSING OF THE DAY...

Lord, I said to the one who hurt me, "I forgive you," and I thought I meant it. When something calls up the pain I thought I had banished once and for all, please remind me that Your son didn't keep a tally of his stripes or a count of the thorns that pierced his head.

Help me release the shock and anger that still make their way into my darkest thoughts. Teach me the ways of peace of mind after peace has been shattered.

Jody Serey

April 27

ONE LESSON I HAVE LEARNED IN MY LIFE IS...

Churches need to change. The numbers of people who are attending church continue to decline. And, although America remains one of the most spiritual countries in the world, there is no doubt that except for some mega-churches, Christianity is in decline in the United States.

Of course, the question is "why?" Some say we have become too materialistic as a society. Some say the message of the church has become irrelevant to younger people. And, others say, religion has become too much about money. In a wonderful book called The Prodigal God, author Tim Keller says there are basically two kinds of people in the world: Pharisees and sinners. He goes on to say that based on the story of the two sons and the Prodigal Father, "…if our churches aren't appealing to younger brothers, they must be more full of elder brothers than we'd like to think." What he means is pretty clear: the folks in our churches have become more judgmental and less welcoming of sinners.

Churches need to reflect God. And the only way that will happen is if we all recognize we need God's mercy and begin to rejoice when a brother or a sister receives it. Then churches can become places where all of us share in the banquet the Father throws when the Prodigal Son returns.

PRAYER FOR THE BLESSING OF THE DAY…

Lord, today I pray for my church community.
May we always be a place of welcome and mercy.
May our Sunday service overflow with the unconditional love of God.
And may we celebrate with all who come home. AMEN.

Fr. Dale

April 28

ONE LESSON I HAVE LEARNED IN MY LIFE IS…

Pride is very un-becoming. Of course we are proud of our children, our nation, and our community. But that is a different kind of pride. Being proud of someone else puts the focus on them and it is a good thing. But a proud-self -- always putting the focus on self or self-accomplishments -- is unhealthy. The book of Proverbs (11:2) says "When pride comes, then comes disgrace; but wisdom is with the humble." True humility recognizes God as the source of all talents and accomplishments. It counts all accomplishments as God's blessing!

71

PRAYER FOR THE BLESSING OF THE DAY…

Lord, may I be blessed today. And may I realize that every good thing in my life is a gift and a blessing from You. AMEN.

Fr. Dale

April 29

ONE LESSON I HAVE LEARNED IN MY LIFE IS…

That after you have been hurt, trust is very hard. On a surface level, we have to trust others. Every time we come to a traffic light, we have to trust others to stop at a red light. When we get on a plane, we have to trust the pilot and the crew. But trusting our hearts to others is much harder.

The word trust is like the word true. When we trust someone, we have confidence that they will be true -- that is, they will do what they have promised.

If we don't trust anyone, we will be lonely and bitter people. We may need to be more careful of whom we trust, but without trust you cannot have a real relationship. The same is true with God. We must learn to trust Him, and trust that He loves and cares for us. Sometimes people feel like God has let them down or has hurt them. He never does. At the time we may not understand why things happen. But God is always TRUE to His promise to love us.

PRAYER FOR THE BLESSING OF THE DAY…

Psalm 56:3-4

"When I am afraid, I put my trust in God, whose word I praise, in God I trust, I shall not be afraid. What can flesh do to me?" AMEN.

Fr. Dale

April 30

ONE LESSON I HAVE LEARNED IN MY LIFE IS…

"Heart for the house." This is a saying that was taught to me by a worship pastor and it has stuck with me through the years. What he meant by this was that, when it comes to church ministry, no ministry is more important than the other; they all work together to achieve the same goal, which is loving and serving others like Christ did for us. For me, I took this a step further and looked outside the church. I looked at this as a lifestyle change that started in my heart and impacted everything and everyone around me. Now, whenever I get caught up in my own world, preoccupied with my own agenda, this saying, "Heart for the house" reminds me of what Christian ministry should be.

Having a heart for the house means dying to your own will and doing what is best to further the Kingdom of God. It means parking on the far side of the parking lot on a Sunday morning so that someone else who might not be as agile can park closer. It means holding the door open for a stranger, smiling when you are stuck waiting in a long line at the grocery store, or even letting someone go ahead of you at the bank. When you focus on what you can do to help people around you, you are demonstrating Christ-like love for your community. We need to be a community that cares for each other and reaches out to those who are hurting. We need to be actively asking God, "How can I make a difference today?" When we have a heart for the house we are letting God change our hearts and transform our lives into beacons for His glory.

PRAYER FOR THE BLESSING OF THE DAY...

God, help me to focus on others and how I can show Your love to them. Help me to be cooperative and considerate in everything I do. Let me be the light in the dark, reaching the lost and hurting in my community. And God, help me to have a heart for the house. AMEN.

David Person

May 1

ONE LESSON I HAVE LEARNED IN MY LIFE IS...

We all need encouragement. So, I am writing today to encourage you. The Bible tells us to "encourage one another to love and to do good deeds" (Hebrews 10:24). Consider yourself encouraged!

Life takes us places we never expect. And sometimes the place it takes us is a roller coaster. Life goes up. Life goes down. But, no matter which direction we are facing on any given day, we can always love, hope, do good, and know that God never lets go of us.

PRAYER FOR THE BLESSING OF THE DAY...

I trust You, Lord. I know You desire only good in my life. No matter what happens today, I can be at peace, because You are with me. AMEN.

Fr. Dale

May 2

ONE LESSON I HAVE LEARNED IN MY LIFE IS...

There is no expiration date on an act of kindness. A single simple gesture is remembered indefinitely. It is a prayer, an anointing, and can be a seed of salvation.

PRAYER FOR THE BLESSING OF THE DAY...

Lord, help me to move through my life with my senses tuned to the ones who have stumbled, or stopped moving. Let me never be complacent, or judgmental. Prevent me from becoming smug, content with what I have or who I have become. AMEN.

Jody Serey

May 3

ONE LESSON I HAVE LEARNED IN MY LIFE IS...

There are three goals:
Feel good.
Be good.
Do good.

PRAYER FOR THE BLESSING OF THE DAY...

The past has no power over the present moment. May the entire universe be filled with peace and joy, love and light. May all beings everywhere be happy and free. In some way, may I contribute to that happiness and freedom for all.

Heather Kieny Bergen

May 4

ONE LESSON I HAVE LEARNED IN MY LIFE IS...

We have to pray for bitter people. We all know someone who because of their life experiences has become bitter and angry. People like this are hard to be with because they become toxic and hurt everyone around them.

When we meet someone who is bitter, we have two basic options: flight or fight. In other words, we can do our best to run and get away from them. Or, we can stay in there and hope we can make a positive impact on them.

It is especially hard to deal with a bitter person when they are in our own family. It's hard to get away from a parent, grandparent, or sibling who has become extremely negative.

If we know someone like this, we can do three things. First, we can pray for them. Second, we can make sure they do not impact how we handle life. And, third, we can be kind but honest with them about how they are impacting others.

PRAYER FOR THE BLESSING OF THE DAY...

Ephesians 4:31

"Do not be bitter or angry or mad. Never shout angrily or say things to hurt others. Never do anything evil." AMEN.

Fr. Dale

May 5

ONE LESSON I HAVE LEARNED IN MY LIFE IS...

A life without real meaning is hard to live. When we are young, those familiar sayings about living with a purpose don't seem relevant to us. We just live. As we get older, we want to understand more. Why are we here? Why is there suffering? In the classic book Man's Search For Meaning, Viktor Frankl says that suffering allows us to "transform personal tragedy into a triumph, to turn one's predicament into a human achievement."

I believe the meaning of life is simple; it is to learn how to live. And, even suffering provides that opportunity to love instead of turning bitter.

PRAYER FOR THE BLESSING OF THE DAY...

God, allow this day to be filled with meaning. Let me see things in a new light. Take away my bitterness and fear. Let me choose to LOVE no matter what events take place. I love You, Lord. AMEN.

Fr. Dale

May 6

ONE LESSON I HAVE LEARNED IN MY LIFE IS...

Grief has different aspects. Today I am crying not for the loss of my spouse, but for me -- because it hurts so much. It sounds so selfish. I still miss my husband, but I do know he is not suffering anymore and is rejoicing in God's presence. I also know I will get through this. It is a process and God is with me.

PRAYER FOR THE BLESSING OF THE DAY...

Dear Lord, it hurts so much. Sometimes worse than others. Sometimes gut-wrenching, despair, hurt. Please help me through this. I know You haven't abandoned me, but yet I don't feel Your presence. I know my beloved is in heaven with You rejoicing. Please help me see the Light, the Peace, the Hope. In Jesus' name. AMEN.

2 Corinthians 12:9 "My grace is sufficient for you, for my power is made perfect in weakness."

Camille Heiniger

May 7

ONE LESSON I HAVE LEARNED IN MY LIFE IS...

We should pray the psalms a lot more often. In so many ways, they are perfect prayers. The psalms are filled with human emotion, praise of God, and hope for the future. Jews and Christians have prayed these prayers for nearly 3,000 years. And most important, Jesus himself prayed their very words. I recently found this great quote about the psalms from St. Augustine.

"The Psalm is spoken in the person of our Lord Jesus Christ, in the person of our Lord Jesus Christ, both head and members…He is the head, we are the members. Nor without good reason then, his voice is ours and our voice is also his. Let us therefore listen to the Psalm and recognize in it the voice of Christ."

PRAYER FOR THE BLESSING OF THE DAY…

(Psalm 15)

Lord, who shall be admitted to Your tent
and dwell on Your holy mountain?

He who walks without fault;
he who acts with justice
And speaks the truth from his heart;
he who does not slander with his tongue;

He who does no wrong to his brother,
who casts no slur on his neighbor,
Who holds the godless in disdain,
But honors those who fear the Lord;

Fr. Dale

May 8

ONE LESSON I HAVE LEARNED IN MY LIFE IS…

If I've forgotten that I own it, it's probably time to give it away.

PRAYER FOR THE BLESSING OF THE DAY…

Lord, teach me the difference between saving for a rainy day, and accumulating more things than I could ever possibly need. Encourage me to live fully by living simply, and directing my emotional attachments to people, and not objects.

Jody Serey

May 9

ONE LESSON I HAVE LEARNED IN MY LIFE IS...

Possessions are not as important as I thought they were. In fact the best possessions are ones that we give away. Mother Teresa gave me a beautiful rosary. I put it in a display case in my office. A friend, visiting from New York asked if she could touch it. As she did, she started praying. It was clear what I was supposed to do. Give it to her. I never thought of actually using it; I saw it more as a prized possession. It would have been wrong of me to keep it.

By definition, a possession is something I own or have control over. But when I realize that nothing is mine and all things belong to God -- I become free to let go of things. That is the only way I can make sure that things don't start to own me.

PRAYER FOR THE BLESSING OF THE DAY...

(Matthew 6: 19-21)

"Do not lay up for yourselves treasures on earth, where moth and rust destroy and where thieves break in and steal, but lay up for yourselves treasures in heaven, where neither moth nor rust destroys and where thieves do not break in and steal. For where your treasure is, there your heart will be also."

Fr. Dale

May 10

ONE LESSON I HAVE LEARNED IN MY LIFE IS...

One of my favorite scriptures is Isaiah 40:31, "Those who hope in the LORD will renew their strength. They will soar on wings like eagles; they will run and not grow weary, they will walk and not be faint."

These words lift me up and keep me from growing weary as I wait on the Lord. It's one of my favorite verses because it was one of my dad's favorites.

Daddy was a pastor, and I can still hear his voice when I read the words. His "preacher" voice was louder than his normal speaking voice. He could emphasize words like HOPE, RENEW, SOAR and RUN in a way that would make you sit up and listen! Dad was an encourager by nature, and HOPE was one of his favorite sermon topics. I'm sure those early lessons on hope built the foundation on which I stand today -- having learned how to patiently hope and wait on the LORD for whatever need is on my heart.

Some translations of this verse use the word wait in place of hope: "Those who wait on the Lord shall renew their strength..." For me, it's the same thing. Waiting on the Lord's provision IS the HOPE I have in him. It is my "confident expectation" that He will bring about a specific result, according to His will. I may not know for sure when or how it will happen, but God knows. His thoughts are higher than my thoughts. HE KNOW. And so I wait -- and I hope -- trusting confidently in Him.

PRAYER FOR THE BLESSING OF THE DAY...

Almighty God, thank You for Your faithfulness. Because You love me, You provide for all of my needs. Because You are all-seeing, You hear my heart-cries. Help me to be patient as I wait for You to make Your will to be done in my life. No matter what happens, Lord, I will trust in You and glorify You in the outcome. AMEN.

(Micah 7:7) As for me, I look to the LORD for help. I wait confidently for God to save me, and my God will certainly hear me

Cheryl Armstrong

May 11

ONE LESSON I HAVE LEARNED IN MY LIFE IS...

It is not that "cool" to be "cool". Growing up it seemed like being part of the cool group was important. Even as a young clergyman, I wanted the teens to see me as the "with it" pastor. At this point in my life, I am not even sure what is "in" and what is "out." What I do know is this, that at some point we have to decide to be authentic. If it's cool, great. If it's not so hot, that's okay too. I need to be true to my values, my style, my personality, and to the person God made me to be. I think "authenticity" is the new cool. Once we believe that, we all have the possibility of being the "new cool."

PRAYER FOR THE BLESSING OF THE DAY...

Lord, You made me who I am. Teach me to love and accept myself knowing my only goal should be to please You. AMEN.

Fr. Dale

May 12

ONE LESSON I HAVE LEARNED IN MY LIFE IS...

I thank God each day that I have been born to MY special parents, in the country and place where I have been born and lived my life. I was privileged to travel to Germany this summer for a family reunion with twenty-four other American cousins to meet for the first time. Relatives that I did not even know I had were there, and I walked in my ancestors' footsteps through farms and churches that are still standing five generations later. They told us of their terrible experiences during World War II, and we visited the memorials to those that gave their lives. I felt blessed to be made aware of these roots and know of their deep faith.

Riding on a bus through Vienna, I observed this graffiti printed in bold letters on a closed store window. "WHEN THE POWER OF LOVE OVERCOMES THE LOVE OF POWER, THE WORLD WILL BE AT PEACE." It seemed so fitting that I should chance to see this during this trip and at this time in my life.

When I watch the morning news, this graffiti comes to mind with each reporting of shootings, unwanted immigrants, the competition by candidates for political office, and domestic violence. The Power of Love needs few words.

PRAYER FOR THE BLESSING OF THE DAY...

Psalm 29:11

The Lord will give strength to his people; The Lord will bless his people with peace.

Charlotte Greene

May 13

ONE LESSON I HAVE LEARNED IN MY LIFE IS...

Life doesn't always go the way we plan it. Rain interrupts our picnics, traffic jams make us late, and major events turn our lives upside down.

My life was turned upside down. I lost my home, my job, my friends, and 30 years of very hard work. I also lost my dreams and the plans I had for my life. But in the midst of all that, I also learned a tremendous lesson. That is, that God's plans are much better than mine. And when I embrace His way I will find peace.

PRAYER FOR THE BLESSING OF THE DAY...

Father, in the prophet Isaiah (55:8-9) You tell us, "For my thoughts are nothing like Your thoughts. And my ways are far beyond anything You could imagine." Lord let me accept Your ways. Make this a day of inner peace and deep trust in YOU." AMEN.

Fr. Dale

May 14

ONE LESSON I HAVE LEARNED IN MY LIFE IS...

We do not really understand the Holy Spirit. Somehow the third person of the TRINITY always seems like an afterthought.

The Holy Spirit is God. It is the presence of the Holy Spirit in each of us that makes us a temple of God. And because the Holy Spirit dwells in us, we have power and gifts far beyond what we think we have. The Spirit gives us courage, wisdom, and strength.

Many years ago when I first heard of the charismatic movement, the Spirit movement, it scared me. I heard people praying in tongues and acting in what appeared to be silly ways. Now, all I know is I want to be more aware of the Spirit in my life. I am not frightened by the Spirit; I am dependent on it!

PRAYER FOR THE BLESSING OF THE DAY...

Lord, as Pentecost approaches, I pray for a new Pentecost for our church, our world, and for myself. Come, Holy Spirit. AMEN.

Fr. Dale

May 15

ONE LESSON I HAVE LEARNED IN MY LIFE IS...

Never pull that little thread on your button right before your job interview.

PRAYER FOR THE BLESSING OF THE DAY...

Lord, be with me through the small disasters that threaten the events of the day. If I make a mistake, help me figure out a way to fix what I have broken. I ask You to counter my imperfections with perfect love, and to help me be more complete at the end of the day than I was at the beginning.

Jody Serey

May 16

ONE LESSON I HAVE LEARNED IN MY LIFE IS...

Although many people have "wisdom", it is a hard thing to share. Many times we can't obtain wisdom until we go through some tough times. Knowing that, here are a few good quotes that can make us all a little wise -- if we let them.

"Don't let our happiness depend on something you may lose." (C.S. Lewis)

"Strong people don't put others down...they lift them up." (Michael P. Watson)

"Be wise enough to walk away from the nonsense around you." (Unknown)

"Make good use of opportunity you have." (Ephesians)

A negative mind will never get you a positive life." (Unknown)

PRAYER FOR THE BLESSING OF THE DAY...

Lord, I ask for the gift of wisdom. Please help me to learn from my mistakes and experiences. Open my heart to learn from others, too. AMEN.

Fr. Dale

May 17

ONE LESSON I HAVE LEARNED IN MY LIFE IS...

There are different levels of friendship. In other words, not all friends are created equal. It is certainly good to be friendly to everyone. And beyond that, there will be those we socialize with and share common interests. But the inner circle of three to six people is made of folks who are real friends. They are the companions on the journey of life who walk through the storms with us. From time to time, that inner circle may change. But those people are true gifts from God.

PRAYER FOR THE BLESSING OF THE DAY...

(Take a moment to picture your inner circle, the real friends that have touched your life.)

Thank you, Lord, for the gift of friends. The companions remind me I am never alone. Thank you for being present in my life through them. AMEN.

Fr. Dale

May 18

ONE LESSON I HAVE LEARNED IN MY LIFE IS...

Our world is in turmoil because of wars. Thousands of Christians are being put to death because they won't renounce their faith. History of a thousand years ago is repeating itself by death and destruction of cities and churches, and mass migration of millions of hungry families trying to escape death and destruction.

PRAYER FOR THE BLESSING OF THE DAY...

Lord, we need Your help to overcome the heartache and to help the needy.

(Psalm 37:5)

Trust in the Lord. Commit your way to the Lord like Israel's ancestors, who trusted in God and were rescued.

Bob Greene

May 19

ONE LESSON I HAVE LEARNED IN MY LIFE IS...

Taking a walk is a really good thing. Doctors constantly encourage us to walk and to exercise. But the truth is, it is not just a good thing for our health, it's a GOD thing for our souls.

I'm not sure why, but walking seems to open us up to God. One of my deepest prayer experiences happened one night for me. I was encouraged to think of the cool air as God's love. As it hit my skin and I breathed it in, I was overwhelmed with God's presence. Take some time today, and go for a walk with God!

PRAYER FOR THE BLESSING OF THE DAY...

Lord, throughout the bible we hear of those who walked humbly and faithfully with You. In Genesis, we are told that Noah was a righteous person and that "Noah walked with God." (Genesis 6:9).

I pray I can walk with You today. Let me take time to simply be with You and to remember You are with me each step of my journey. AMEN.

Fr. Dale

May 20

ONE LESSON I HAVE LEARNED IN MY LIFE IS...

A fairly unknown mystic from the 14th century said one of the greatest phrases of all time. Julian of Norwich said, "All shall be well." What a great mantra to keep saying when you are in the midst of a crisis. And what a great outlook to have on life.

Julian was probably a nun, but that is not known for sure. What we do know is that she likely lost her family to the plague prior to living in a convent. She herself almost died, but during her illness she had visions of Jesus. She is considered to be the first woman to write a book in English and her writings continue to survive today.

During one of her visions, Jesus spoke tenderly to Julian. And Jesus told her that despite sin in the world, "All shall be well." It was an incredible moment of compassion.

84

We need to remember these words each day. In the midst of stress, anxiety, tiredness, and even death, "All shall be well."

PRAYER FOR THE BLESSING OF THE DAY...

I trust You, Jesus. "All shall be well." AMEN.

Fr. Dale

May 21

ONE LESSON I HAVE LEARNED IN MY LIFE IS...

I spend a lot of money on things I don't need to spend it on. I don't make a lot of money, but have enough to stop at Starbucks, buy something in the grocery store that looks good and to add another cross to my collection from time to time. None of these are bad or wasteful. But, none of these are really necessary either.

There is an old saying, "Live simply so others may simply live." I need to take that to heart. There are many people throughout the world, and in our own country, that have nothing. By disciplining myself a "little more," I can help others a "little more."

I know I don't respond well to the TV commercials and mailings that I get regarding world hunger. Guilt is not a good motivation for me. But recognizing how blessed I am motivates me to want to share my blessings with others.

PRAYER FOR THE BLESSING OF THE DAY...

(Proverbs 19:17)

"Whoever is generous to the poor, lends to the Lord, and the Lord himself will repay him for his deed." AMEN.

Fr. Dale

May 22

ONE LESSON I HAVE LEARNED IN MY LIFE IS...

Getting out into creation is always good. Somehow when we get out into the mountains, trees, or the water, it is much easier to feel the presence of God. It is always like meeting an artist through an amazing piece of artwork. The great writer C.S. Lewis said, "No philosophical theory which I have come across is a radical improvement on the words of Genesis, that 'In the beginning, God made Heaven and Earth'. The only words I can add to that -- wow, how generous God is to share His Heaven and His Earth with us."

PRAYER FOR THE BLESSING OF THE DAY...

(Psalm 148)

Praise the Lord!

Praise the Lord from the heavens;
   praise him in the heights above.
Praise him, all his angels;
   praise him, all his heavenly hosts.
Praise him, sun and moon;
   praise him, all you shining stars.
Praise him, you highest heavens
   and you waters above the skies.

Let them praise the name of the Lord,
   for at his command they were created.

Fr. Dale

May 23

ONE LESSON I HAVE LEARNED IN MY LIFE IS...

We cannot underestimate the power of the Holy Spirit. The bible says if we have faith, we can move mountains. Many local people have interpreted that to mean that Camelback Mountain could be moved somewhere else. But what it really means is that God's spirit can break down a mountain of hatred, a hill of misunderstanding, and can fill in a valley of doubt. In baptism we have all been given a share of the Holy Spirit. If we all used it, the Spirit could change the world.

PRAYER FOR THE BLESSING OF THE DAY...

Come Holy Spirit, come and fill this day with Your love, Your prayer, and Your passion. May I open my heart to You today and may I use Your strength to make the world a more loving place. AMEN.

Fr. Dale

May 24

ONE LESSON I HAVE LEARNED IN MY LIFE IS...

We should be thankful for God's mercy. Being raised from birth as Catholic, I was always taught that the key to greater understanding was "The Fear of God", or "Fear of the Lord."As a child, I never understood this. I always thought that if we had a loving, compassionate, and merciful God, why should we be afraid? So, I looked to the bible for answers.

A particular psalm stood out, Psalm 111:10, and it says, "The fear of the LORD is the beginning of wisdom; all who follow His precepts have good understanding. To Him belongs eternal praise." So, the bible is saying that if I fear the Lord and follow all His rules and praise Him, I will have the beginning of wisdom. But, as clear cut as that was, I still didn't understand the concept.

So, I read the bible some more. And, a story in the bible helped me to understand why I should "fear" God. The story of Sodom and Gomorrah, in Genesis 19. In verses 15-17, it says the city is being punished for its outcries against the Lord. And the angels tell Lot, "With the coming of dawn, the angels urged Lot, saying, 'Hurry! Take your wife and your two daughters who are here, or you will be swept away when the city is punished.' When he hesitated, the men grasped his hand and the hands of his wife and of his two daughters and led them safely out of the city, for the Lord was merciful to them. As soon as they had brought them out, one of them said, 'Flee for your lives! Don't look back, and don't stop anywhere in the plain! Flee to the mountains or you will be swept away!'"

And in verses 24-26, it describes what happened to the town, "Then the Lord rained down burning sulfur on Sodom and Gomorrah—from the Lord out of the heavens. Thus He overthrew those cities and the entire plain, destroying all those living in the cities -- and also the vegetation in the land. But Lot's wife looked back, and she became a pillar of salt."

It clearly explains that those who are against the Lord will be punished, and with those kind of capabilities I would fear anyone who had them. I began to understand the concept, but with more understanding came more thankfulness for the Lord's mercy towards me and my family. I was thankful that I was receiving love and compassion, and that I could follow the Lord.

PRAYER FOR THE BLESSING OF THE DAY...

Thank Lord for this beautiful day, and thank You for bestowing Your never ending mercy to me and those around me. You are truly an awesome God. AMEN.

Peter Rehm-Gerdes

May 25

ONE LESSON I HAVE LEARNED IN MY LIFE IS...

Worship is about the most important thing we do. Worship isn't just a Sunday thing, but our best worship should be on Sunday as a community. A great Christian preacher named A.W. Tozer talks about how our church worship must be ALIVE. He equates a dead man with the many dead churches we have in our world. Tozer says, "It is literally true that some churches are dead. The Holy Spirit has gone out of them and all you have left are the remains."

We must always bring life and spirit to our Sunday community gatherings.

PRAYER FOR THE BLESSING OF THE DAY...

"Lord, send Your Holy Spirit in power, that we might not be a dead church, striving to look alive, pretending to function as though alive, while the life is actually gone." AMEN.

(A.W. Tozer)

Fr. Dale

May 26

ONE LESSON I HAVE LEARNED IN MY LIFE IS...

Everyone wants to avoid pain. It's interesting to watch people in the hospital be asked, "What is your level of pain between one and ten?"

The answer to that is so subjective, only the person knows what is being felt and how bad it is. Yet we have one thing in common: pain is something to be avoided or ended.

There are different types of pain. Some pain is physical and some is emotional. Physical pain is our body's way of telling us something is wrong. Emotional pain tells us that some relationship isn't right. Emotional pain can also come with grief or anxiety.

God knows when we are in pain. He doesn't enjoy watching us hurt. He wants to relieve us of pain and hurts, yet He knows that it is also part of the human condition. His own son experienced both physical and emotional pain. The most important thing for us to know is that God never walks away from us when we are hurting. When pain or suffering strike, we have to put our trust and confidence in God and not give up.

PRAYER FOR THE BLESSING OF THE DAY...

(Isaiah 41:10)

"Do not be afraid, for I am with you. Don't be discouraged, for I am Your God. I will strengthen you and help you. I will hold you up with my victorious right hand." AMEN.

Fr. Dale

May 27

ONE LESSON I HAVE LEARNED IN MY LIFE IS...

A four-year-old will cut her own bangs an hour before the appointment for your family photos. And years later, that will be your favorite picture of her.

PRAYER FOR THE BLESSING OF THE DAY...

Lord, let me remember with a smile and not with anger. Help me push aside the criticism of others who do not love what I love, or honor what I honor. Let me treasure what is precious to me without having my joy diminished by those who cannot tell the difference between diamonds and glass.

Jody Serey

May 28

ONE LESSON I HAVE LEARNED IN MY LIFE IS...

Memorial Day is a very sacred day. Many people confuse Memorial Day with Veterans Day. Veterans Day honors those who have served in our military. Memorial Day honors and remembers those who have given their lives so that America could be free.

The history of Memorial Day dates back to after the Civil War. It was originally called "Decoration Day" because people would go to the cemetery and decorate the graves of those who died in the armed forces.

None of us likes war. And we are all called to pray for peace and to end violence throughout the world. But when a nation goes to war, the ones who make the ultimate sacrifice need to be honored. And, we should never forget to pray for the families of those who have died. They too, make an incredible sacrifice of growing up without a father or mother, losing a spouse, or burying their own children.

PRAYER FOR THE BLESSING OF THE DAY...

(John 15:13)

"There is no greater love than to lay down one's life for one's friends." AMEN.

Fr. Dale

May 29

ONE LESSON I HAVE LEARNED IN MY LIFE IS...

One of the BEST quotes in scripture comes from the book of Micah. Micah was a minor prophet who was a contemporary of the well-known prophets Isaiah, Amos, Hosea. He writes a very simple directive to the people of Israel as he teaches them to honor the sovereignty of Yahweh. Micah says (Micah 6:8) "He has told you, O Mortal, what is good; and what does the Lord require of you, but to do justice, and to love kindness, and to walk humbly with your God."

To me, Micah says it so simply. Be just, be kind. Walk in humility and simplicity. Honor God above all else. If we can do those simple things, we are on the road to a heavenly life.

PRAYER FOR THE BLESSING OF THE DAY...

[Micah (6:8) (Message Bible Translation)]

"But he's already made it plain how to live, what to do,
what God is looking for in men and women.
It's quite simple: Do what is fair and just to your neighbor,
be compassionate and loyal in your love,
And don't take yourself too seriously —
take God seriously."

Fr. Dale

May 30

ONE LESSON I HAVE LEARNED IN MY LIFE IS...

Be thankful for those soldiers who have died serving their country. This week is Memorial Day, a time for all of us to remember the soldiers and their families who have made a sacrifice for our freedom of speech, travel, assembly, prayer, choice of career, and our freedom to live wherever we choose to live and to worship God. I learned a long time ago that freedom is not free. There is a cost. Almost 1,137,237 men and women have died in service to their country since the Revolutionary War to ensure that we are free people today. May we never forget that and take a moment or two to say a prayer of thanks.

PRAYER FOR THE BLESSING OF THE DAY...

EVERYDAY IS MEMORIAL DAY

Today we remember
A grateful nation recalls
Our Men and Women
Who paid the price
Of freedom for us all

For those of us who
Served beside them
Every day is Memorial Day
We can't let their memories fade

We were touched by their loss

Their lives touched ours
Changing and helping us
Becoming who we are
Grateful for what we have
Freedom at Home

For those left at home
You gave us your sons and daughters
Husbands and wives
Fathers and mothers
Brothers and sisters
Friends and lovers
Thank you for sharing them with us

We miss them all
We won't let them be forgot
That is why each of us
Who have been in battle knows
We can never ever forget
That every day is Memorial Day

(Copyright May 30, 2004 by Kerry "Doc" Pardue)

May 31

ONE LESSON I HAVE LEARNED IN MY LIFE IS...

No matter how long I live on the desert, the heat sneaks up unexpectedly. Why do I not remember to appreciate the days and nights of true beauty, and not fill up the softest days with things that don't matter?

PRAYER FOR THE BLESSING OF THE DAY...

Lord, I am a waster of time and opportunity. When there is a cool breeze, I tend to shut the window to avoid being distracted.

Help push me into the sunlight while my flesh can still appreciate it. Pull my eyes upwards towards a sky made blue by all things wonderful. And when the summer comes to the desert again, fill my heart with gratitude for shade, water, and the privilege of facing another season.

Jody Serey

June 1

ONE LESSON I HAVE LEARNED IN MY LIFE IS...

Old friendships don't happen overnight. They are the result of fidelity, forgiveness, and the honor of sharing history. Jesus said, "I call you friends."

PRAYER FOR THE BLESSING OF THE DAY...

Lord, please keep mine from ever being the one voice that was longed for, but remained silent. Lead me back to the ones who thought I had abandoned them when my own concerns made me distant. If my voice was ever raised in anger, let my head be lowered as I ask to be forgiven.

Jody Serey

June 2

ONE LESSON I HAVE LEARNED IN MY LIFE IS...

That laughter is a good thing. Back when I used to read the newspaper one of the first things I would turn to was the cartoon "Family Circus." I knew the creator, Bil Keane, and knowing him somehow made the cartoons funnier. I remember one cartoon where little Billy told his dad that he knew God's first name. His dad was somewhat confused. And Billy answered his name is "Andy." Then he started singing, "Andy walks with me, Andy talks with me, Andy tells me I am His own."

We can find humor in almost anything. Comedians tell us that it's all about perspective. Some say it's the art of combining the expected and unexpected.

I have found that laughter unites people, breaks the ice in tense or new situations, and makes strangers feel at home. I know God isn't human, but somehow I believe He enjoys a good laugh also. He must! He keeps people like you and me around.

PRAYER FOR THE BLESSING OF THE DAY...

Lord, let me laugh today. Give me a deep sense of joy and hope. AMEN.

Fr. Dale

June 3

ONE LESSON I HAVE LEARNED IN MY LIFE IS...

We focus on our problems way too much. We give them tremendous power over us. Our problems often control our moods, choices, and reactions. Problems are real. They need to be worked on, but we don't need to obsess over them.

I heard someone say, "Talking about our problems is our greatest addiction. Break the habit and start talking about your joys."

It's great advice, but breaking the problem addiction is going to take some work.

Perhaps the best thing to do is to get the people in our inner circle to work on this together. Accountability is needed to break any addiction. If those close to us remind us to "kindly get more positive" it would help. Maybe we can do that for someone else, as well.

Focusing on our blessings and joys can only help make our day better.

PRAYER FOR THE BLESSING OF THE DAY...

Lord, make me a grateful person. Help me to see the many blessings You have given to me and to stop worrying as much as I do about the challenges in my life. AMEN.

Fr. Dale

June 4

ONE LESS I HAVE LEARNED IN MY LIFE IS...

There is no hierarchy when it comes to the pets we love.

I learned this when I accepted a "feeder fish" that had somehow dodged its intended fate as food for larger fish in an aquarium, only to be abandoned in somebody's office cubicle after a lay-off. I took in the little goldfish, named him "Bob," and proceeded to get attached to him over the course of almost a decade.

Bob grew considerably, and was so tame that he would swim up to the top of his little tank, and wait for treats. We thought he might like something to play with, so we bought him a small glass fish that floated, and he pulled it around on a string that hung down.

And then, over the course of a few weeks, Bob died. We did everything we knew to do to help him survive, but he had other ideas.

So, the little glass floating fish has a place of honor on the Christmas tree every year, and we remember a goldfish that proved that love is love, no matter where it finds itself residing.

PRAYER FOR THE BLESSING OF THE DAY...

Lord, thank you for all the ways You have provided us to find love and joy in Your creations. Let me be a good steward of the things of the earth that walk, run, fly, crawl, and swim. AMEN.

Jody Serey

June 5

ONE LESSON I HAVE LEARNED IN MY LIFE IS...

We all have to keep learning. As a kid, I couldn't wait to graduate into high school. In high school, I couldn't wait to graduate into college. Somehow, graduation represented some goal, some end I longed for. Now that I am older, I wish I had paid more attention in school because now I look for opportunities to learn. I realize I am not as smart as I thought I was. I need to keep learning, keep reading, keep going to workshops, and asking questions. There are so many people skills, life skills, and great information I have not learned. Today seems like a good day to learn some new things.

PRAYER FOR THE BLESSING OF THE DAY...

Lord, You are all-knowing, all-loving, and all-merciful. Allow me to share in Your knowledge, be an example of Your love, and an instrument of Your mercy. AMEN.

Fr. Dale

June 6

ONE LESSON I HAVE LEARNED IN MY LIFE IS...

In order to spread the Gospel, we need to talk less and love more. As a preacher, that is hard for me to admit. I always think if I can only add a few more thoughts, I can change a few hearts. The comedian George Burns gave his opinion about a good sermon. He said, "The secret of a good sermon is to have a good beginning and a good ending, and to have the two as close together as possible."

St. Francis of Assisi said the same thing...well, almost the same thing. He said "to preach the Gospel always, and if necessary, use words." Generally speaking, hearts are not changed by thoughts or words; they are changed by experiencing love in action.

Jesus preached. But he also healed, fed, consoled, and spent time with sinners. As Christians, we need to always be conscious of the call we have to be a light to a sometimes very dark world.

PRAYER FOR THE BLESSING OF THE DAY...

Father, by my example and attitude, I pray that today I may touch someone with Your love. AMEN.

Fr. Dale

June 7

ONE LESSON I HAVE LEARNED IN MY LIFE IS...

As we get older, the months, the seasons, and the years pass more quickly. To me when I was a young person, it seemed like hours and days went by very fast. But a year seemed like a lifetime. As I get older, days seem a little longer. But, before I know it, it is summer again. I know time doesn't change, but clearly our perception does.

God is timeless. In Him, there are no minutes or years. Maybe in some way God helps us to change our perception of time in order to prepare us for eternity. All I know is this -- the best thing I can do now is to put JOY into every moment, every day, every season, and every year. Who knows how many more any of us may have.

PRAYER FOR THE BLESSING OF THE DAY...

Dear Father,

Thank you for the gift of life and for the time You give us on earth. Help me, today, to embrace each moment with gratitude, laughter and love. AMEN.

Fr. Dale

June 8

ONE LESSON I HAVE LEARNED IN MY LIFE IS...

In reflection, I thought about our first week of marriage in 1960. The thought is how the depth of a love for someone changes over time. When first married, our goals are about preparing for a long future, getting more education, working hard to move ahead, being passionate for each other, and having a "fun" time in life.

Time goes by. A lot of life's experiences take off the sharp edges and your character changes. Hopefully, for the best, and somewhere along the line, if you invite Him -- God finds a place in your heart.

Then those senior years hit. Life really changes. You see life through a new set of eyes. One of you becomes unhealthy and you find out that serving and loving one another finds a whole new depth. Patience, tolerance, and grace become more alive in your character. I pray more. I thank God more, and I cherish those few friends more.

PRAYER FOR THE BLESSING OF THE DAY...

Lord, thank you for the lessons I continue to learn every day. Lead me in Your ways, teach me more patience and understanding. Keep me healthy so that I may complete Your mission You have put in my heart. (Proverbs 2:7-8)

John Null

June 9

ONE LESSON I HAVE LEARNED IN MY LIFE IS...

Thirty-one flavors can be overwhelming. When I go in to the ice cream store and all those choices are there, it can be difficult to decide on one. But not all choices are that complex. When it comes to how I see life, I can choose to be an optimist or a pessimist. As I get older, I choose to be an optimist. Negativity has become less appealing to me. I don't live in denial. I know very well that there are many negative things in life. But focusing on them, and talking about them, doesn't seem to help. I think optimism -- seeing the good and the potential for good -- makes a better choice for my life.

PRAYER FOR THE BLESSING OF THE DAY...

Lord, help me to see the good in others, the good in the world, and the good in me. As I focus on the good, let me thank You, Lord that You are such a good God. AMEN.

Fr. Dale

June 10

ONE LESSON I HAVE LEARNED IN MY LIFE IS...

You have to appreciate the little things. So often we are caught up in the business of life. Between work, grocery shopping, and balancing the checkbook, we can start to lose focus on what really matters. There have been many days when I would come home feeling exhausted and miserable, knowing that tomorrow I had to wake up and go through the same routine all over again. Wake up, work, sleep, and repeat. After a while it wears you down until you reach the critical point and fall apart. I've been at this point more often than I care to admit, and what I've come to realize is that I need to remind myself of the things that make life amazing. For me nothing lifts me out of the mundane routine like nature. Just getting outside, going on a hike, going camping, or a road trip to a new city helps me to reawaken the childlike wonder and appreciation of life. In today's society, we tend to think that once we get that promotion, new job, or a new car or house that we will truly be happy. This is not true. The secret to happiness is contentment and an appreciation for what you have and where you are. Honestly, this isn't always easy. But I find that when you surrender your life, time, possessions, and energy to God and give Him total control, you start to be transformed into a happy and content individual. You don't need money. You don't need fame. You need the love and grace of the one who created you and an appreciation for all he has blessed you with.

PRAYER FOR THE BLESSING OF THE DAY...

God, help me to be content in all things. Help me to take notice of the things You have blessed me with. Help me to dive into the mysteries of the wondrous world You created. And help me appreciate the little things. AMEN.

David Person

June 11

ONE LESSON I HAVE LEARNED IN MY LIFE IS...

You can't hope for eternal life if you can't entertain yourself alone for an hour.

PRAYER FOR THE BLESSING OF THE DAY...

Lord, teach me to love solitude so I can hear Your voice above the noise in my own head. Quiet my thoughts so I can feel the mightiness of Your whisper. Let me know the majesty of Your power in the flash of the tiniest wing, the slightest of the cool breezes.

If You are the Lord of thunder, You are also the Lord of my heartbeat.

Jody Serey

June 12

ONE LESSON I HAVE LEARNED IN MY LIFE IS...

HE IS GOD AND I AM NOT.

Very often in life we are faced with situations and experiences where we forget or ignore that reality. Perhaps it's frustrating relationships with friends or family members. If only they would do or act as we feel appropriate everything would be fine. Really?

Perhaps it's an illness that beleaguers us or a loved one. If only we could work hard enough and find the right treatment or doctor, health would return. As my husband struggled with the increasing ravages of Alzheimer's disease for many years, he never seemed to lose faith that God is in charge. Today, June 12, was his birthday. While we should do all in our power to alleviate the pain and suffering of a situation, we should also remember that, ultimately, it is not all in our power.

PRAYER FOR THE BLESSING OF THE DAY...

May I focus today on the abundance of beauty in our world, remembering the joy there is in hope ; the comfort there is in patience; the peace there is in prayer; the realization that every individual I encounter may be Jesus in disguise.

Be joyful in hope, patient in affliction, faithful in prayer. (Romans 12:12)

Sandy Thiernau

June 13

ONE LESSON I HAVE LEARNED IN MY LIFE IS...

The opinion that other people have of me doesn't really matter. As I say these words, I realize I cannot flippantly disregard how I impact others. But I also realize that I will never be able to please everyone or have everyone like me. I certainly learned this lesson the hard way. At the peak of my religious career, I was humbled and lied about. There was nothing I could do to change the situation.

Spiritual writer Brennan Manning says, "Real freedom is freedom from the opinions of others. Above all, freedom from your opinions about yourself."

In other words, what ultimately matters is God and how He sees us. And deep within my heart I know He sees us as his beloved children.

PRAYER FOR THE BLESSING OF THE DAY...

Thank you, Lord, for loving me unconditionally. Help me to try to please You today and not worry about pleasing others. AMEN.

Fr. Dale

June 14

ONE LESSON I HAVE LEARNED IN MY LIFE IS...

A good marriage happens one moment at a time. So does a bad one.

PRAYER FOR THE BLESSING OF THE DAY...

Lord, help me remember not just my marriage vows, but the Golden Rule. Betrayal does not always wear the face of another person. The harsh word, the thoughtless act may not cut deep enough to kill for many years, but they are small and relentless assassins. Help me be kind when I feel the least like being so. Help me keep from bringing pain and death to the love of the one I swore to love the most forever.

Jody Serey

June 15

ONE LESSON I HAVE LEARNED IN MY LIFE IS...

That summer is here and that means it's time for vacation. I must admit, I am not very good at vacation. I know people do vacations differently (stay-cations, time off, elaborate trips or cruises). And I know people do vacations for different reasons (rest, relaxation, getting away from jobs, seeing new places). But, I suspect in today's high tech world, fewer people really get away. I am writing this in Santa Fe on my annual timeshare vacation. Everywhere I look, folks are on the phone, I-pads, and using computers. It's hard today to really disconnect.

The word vacation comes from the words "to vacate." When we vacate, we are leaving somewhere and going someplace else. I think it is important that we do vacate our daily lives sometimes.

Retired folks also need to be refreshed and get away. Even if it is for a day or weekend, vacating our daily lives gives us a new perspective. So -- however you do it, for however long you go -- let's all make a commitment to do a mentally healthy thing and vacate our normal lives.

PRAYER FOR THE BLESSING OF THE DAY...

Refresh me, Jesus, during these warm months of summer. Help me to find a way to put aside my daily life and retreat into Your creation. AMEN.

Fr. Dale

June 16

ONE LESSON I HAVE LEARNED IN MY LIFE IS...

There is a whole lot of information available in our world. The Internet has so much information that it has closed a number of libraries. But, for all the information, there still is not a whole lot of inspiration. We need more inspiring people, inspiring stories, and inspiring actions. It's helpful to seek out those stories and those people who do inspire. But, it is also helpful to try to do something each day that inspires someone else. We don't need to be Mother Teresa to do something beautiful for God.

PRAYER FOR THE BLESSING OF THE DAY...

Lord, bring someone inspiring into my life today. And please Lord, let me be an inspiration to someone else. AMEN.

Fr. Dale

June 17

ONE LESSON I HAVE LEARNED IN MY LIFE IS...

That the saying "Let them eat cake" is one of the most famous sayings that may have never been said. The story is, that during the reign of Louis XVI in France, the country went into famine. Marie Antoinette responded to the news that the people had no bread and were starving by saying, "Let them eat cake." At least, that was the story. There is no evidence that it ever happened.

From what is known of Marie Antoinette, she was neither ignorant nor callous. And the saying itself is often attributed to someone else who lived 100 years earlier.

Many times we assume the things we hear about people are true. This should be a good lesson that rumors and gossip happen, but it is not

fair to assume it is a fact. Things we read in the newspaper, hear from
neighbors or on the 10:00 p.m. news may indeed be someone's perception and not the truth. It is good for us not to pre-judge anyone by what
others say…even a French monarch.

PRAYER FOR THE BLESSING OF THE DAY…

Father, we are all Your children. Help me to accept each person You
send into my life with an open heart and open mind. AMEN.

Fr. Dale

June 18

ONE LESSON I HAVE LEARNED IN MY LIFE IS…

Be still and listen to the voice of mystery. This is best found in nature
while allowing all thoughts to gradually fall away.

PRAYER FOR THE BLESSING OF THE DAY…

The power of presence be with you today.
Be still and know that I am God (pause and listen)
Be still and know that I am (pause and listen)
Be still and know (pause and listen)
Be still (pause and listen)
Be (pause and listen)

Brad Kuluris

June 19

ONE LESSON I HAVE LEARNED IN MY LIFE IS…

Eating a meal together is not about food.

The one who prepares the meal, and the one who shares it, are each
twice blessed with something to eat, and company that can be shared.
A meal is a respite from both loneliness and hunger.

PRAYER FOR THE BLESSING OF THE DAY…

Lord, let me never take for granted what is on my plate. Make me
thankful for what I eat, and what I drink – and for what nourishes me
from having the company of the ones around my table.

Jody Serey

June 20

ONE LESSON I HAVE LEARNED IN MY LIFE IS...

We all need to get more comfortable with silence, especially in prayer. We live in a loud world. Our days are filled with TV, radio, car alarms, phones, and people talking. Often we bring all that noise into prayer. The great Christian writer A.W. Tozer wrote "that in some instances absolute silence might well become our greatest act of worship."

The book of Revelation says (8:1), "When the Lamb opened the seventh seal, there was silence in Heaven for about half an hour." Maybe that should give us some indication of how we can improve our prayer lives.

There are many different kinds of prayer. Some should involve drums, guitars, some are made up of words, and some should just be silence. God can do amazing things in our hearts when we give him a half an hour to do so.

PRAYER FOR THE BLESSING OF THE DAY...

(Psalm 46:11)

"Be still, and know that I am God. I will be exalted among the nations, I will be exalted on the earth!" AMEN.

Fr. Dale

June 21

ONE LESSON I HAVE LEARNED IN MY LIFE IS...

There is a season for everything. There are seasons of hardship, seasons of joy, seasons of prosperity, and seasons of forced fragility. Throughout all seasons of life, I know only one thing to stay constant, and that is the overwhelming sensation of God's love. I know from personal experience how difficult it can be to truly feel and embrace God's love when times get tough. I've found that we seldom see the love of God in our lives when faced with less than desirable circumstances. The amazing beauty of God's love is that it is constant throughout both the good and the bad seasons of life. So the next time you enter into a season of sadness, suffering, or financial difficulties, look for the subtle touch of God's constant and never ending love.

PRAYER FOR THE BLESSING OF THE DAY...

God, help me to see Your Love, even when life gets me down. Help me to focus on the positive and know that You are with me even in the toughest of seasons. Help me to trust You to give me strength day by day so that I can walk with my head held high, a beacon of Your love – so all can look at me and feel Your love through me. Lead me and guide me, every day of my life. In Your name I pray, AMEN.

David Person

June 22

ONE LESSON I HAVE LEARNED IN MY LIFE IS...

Be grateful to God for the gift of each day.

Thank you, dear God, for the gift of another day. Countless others experience life today, but my experience is unique to me – a reminder that I am unique to You.

Remind me, too, that whatever happens today is already known to You and allowed by You in Your overall plan to draw me to You.

PRAYER FOR THE BLESSING OF THE DAY...

Lord, so I might turn to You and know You are here, grant me the grace to want to grow nearer to You.

Jack Redman

June 23

ONE LESSON I HAVE LEARNED IN MY LIFE IS...

Stress is a killer. It kills the body, the heart, and the human spirit. I don't know when life got so stressful for all of us. I know generations before us had a lot to deal with. I can't imagine how folks made it through the Great Depression or World War II. I do know this, though. Between finances, media, reports of crazy people with guns, and imperfect families -- stress seems very high.

Stress is a form of anxiety and pressure. In many ways, it is the opposite of faith. Jesus says, "Do not let your hearts be troubled. Have faith in God and faith in me." (John 1:1)

We must take Jesus' words to heart. No worry has ever made the world a better place. Nor will it enrich our lives.

PRAYER FOR THE BLESSING OF THE DAY...
(Matthew 6:2-29)

"Consider the lilies of the field, how they grow: they neither toil nor spin, yet I tell you, even Solomon in all his glory was not clothed like one of these."

(Matthew 6:34)

"So do not worry about tomorrow, for tomorrow will bring worries of its own. Today's' trouble is enough for today."

Fr. Dale

June 24

ONE LESSON I HAVE LEARNED IN MY LIFE IS...

One lesson I have learned as I reflect on this date, is from 1960 as I was about to enter a life's commitment through marriage to Sandie on the 25th, and how a young love can grow into a long and large love through trial and forgiveness. That is achieved by bringing struggle and God into that relationship at the beginning and not to wait until God has to handle the mess we can make of it over time. But, we also found out He can clean up anything and make it right through His grace and mercy.

PRAYER FOR THE BLESSING OF THE DAY...

Lord, thank You for entering our lives in spite of our mistakes and selfish ways, for Your patience and relenting love that not only saved our marriage, but our souls from a dark future. Let our daily walk be a witness for the grace and mercy You always make available for those of us who reach out for it. AMEN.

(Proverbs 3:3-4) "Let love and faithfulness never leave you: bind them around your neck, write them on the tablet of your hearts. Then you will win favor and a good name in the sight of God and man."

John & Sandie Null

June 25

ONE LESSON I HAVE LEARNED IN MY LIFE IS...

I am unconditionally loved by God. It is such a simple message you would think I would have always known that. But sometimes, the simplest messages are the hardest to accept. I spent years trying to earn God's love. I worked about as hard as any human being could. Then, after all my work was disposed of -- I was left with the question, "What now?" The answer was simple: let God be who He is and love. In other words, ACCEPT the gift.

My life is different now. And, in many ways it is better. I accept the love that God our Father has for me. I pray you will do the same.

PRAYER FOR THE BLESSING OF THE DAY...

God, Father,

You are the source of all love. And whatever You do -- You do perfectly. Thank you for loving all of us imperfect people. You are an amazing God. Please make this an amazing day by allowing me to accept Your perfect and unconditional gift. AMEN.

Fr. Dale

June 26

ONE LESSON I HAVE LEARNED IN MY LIFE IS...

Cars come with a rear view mirror but people don't. God didn't see fit to equip us with mirrors that help us look back on our lives. That doesn't mean we don't remember our mistakes, but it does mean we can't dwell on what is already past. We can learn from our past, but it doesn't do us any good to try and relive them.

There is a great quote which says, "You can't start the next chapter of your life if you keep re-reading the last one." That says it all!

The future is where we are going. There is a reason God gives us a sunrise each morning to remind us that we begin again. Our future includes today, tomorrow, and eternal life. How good and gracious God is that He puts the past behind and allows us to do the same.

PRAYER FOR THE BLESSING OF THE DAY...

(1 Corinthians 2:9)

"No eye has seen, no ear has heard, no mind has conceived what God has prepared for those who love Him." AMEN.

Fr. Dale

June 27

ONE LESSON I HAVE LEARNED IN MY LIFE IS...

When life seems to be going all wrong, instead of fretting and worrying, I need to trust God. God is in charge of me. He takes the bad and the ugly and works them together for His glory and my good.

[(Romans 8:26-28 The Message (MSG)] Meanwhile, the moment we get tired in the waiting, God's Spirit is right alongside helping us along. If we don't know how or what to pray, it doesn't matter. He does our praying in and for us, making prayer out of our wordless sighs, our aching groans. He knows us far better than we know ourselves, knows our pregnant condition, and keeps us present before God. That's why we can be so sure that every detail in our lives of love for God is worked into something good.

PRAYER FOR THE BLESSING OF THE DAY...

Lord, even when it is hard for me to thank You, I thank You for the hard times. Thank you for teaching me to trust in You no matter what. You hold me tight in Your hands and I am safe. AMEN.

Carol Taylor

June 28

ONE LESSON I HAVE LEARNED IN MY LIFE IS...

Let go and let God. On this day, many years ago a little girl was born. We adopted her at the age of seven months. As we drove home with this little dark haired, blue eyed girl, our lives were enriched in many ways -- but there were hard times as she grew older. Worry was constant. That love surrounded her as a child is still there, deeper than before, no matter what she has done or not done.

The love and trust a child has for its parents is total. That is the kind of trust and love we have in Jesus. God's love is everlasting and envelopes us. Over and over we hear this, but when troubles happen, we start worrying and fussing, forgetting that God is in charge. He is our strength and our peace. We need to let go and let God.

PRAYER FOR THE BLESSING OF THE DAY...

Lord, help me keep You in the front of my life, first in all I think, do and say. Don't let me flounder in my own thought and actions. Lead me, I surrender. Abba, You are the Potter, and we are Your clay.

"Who of you by worrying can add a single hour to his life? Since you cannot do this very little thing, why do you worry about the rest?" (Luke 1:12-26)

Elaine Dube

June 29

ONE LESSON I HAVE LEARNED IN MY LIFE IS...

The feeling of being unwelcome hurts. I went through the experience of being outcast when my own church discarded me. I do not think God intended to make people disposable. But, in reality we dispose of people in many ways. Abortion, giving up on someone, ignoring people, rejecting people we disagree with, and prejudice are all ways we dispose of others. When we dispose of others, we dispose of the God who dwells within them. It is time we value life. And it is time we value each other.

PRAYER FOR THE BLESSING OF THE DAY...

Lord, give me an opportunity today to make someone feel welcome. I know You will be present in each person I contact today. May my heart be open to receiving You and others into my world.

Fr. Dale

June 30

ONE LESSON I HAVE LEARNED IN MY LIFE IS...

It's all about payback. We come into this world, held upside down by our ankles and smacked on our behinds till we cry. From that first out-burst of breath we're dependent on others for our survival until we're able to care for ourselves. We're fed, changed and rocked to sleep those early developmental years until we learn to master these and other tasks on our own. We're content; life is good.

Fast forward twenty years. If we're lucky we've graduated school and are embarking on a life outside our comfort zone. We wonder how we got where we are and at what price to the adults in our lives. Now that we've flown from the nest and cut those ties, now what?

Somewhere along the way, sooner for some than others, we see our path in life is unlike anyone else's. Wow! How unique. The schooling, reading, adult interactions, experiences, teach us something divine has our backs.

Regardless of when this realization knocks us back a few steps if we believe, we must face our obligation to do unto others. Praise, educate, volunteer, sponsor. Do what it takes; it's payback time!

PRAYER FOR THE BLESSING OF THE DAY...

Lord, I pray You never let go of my hand as You continue to lead me day by day down the unique path You paved for me. Let me see Your face in each person I encounter and reach out as You always do to help those in need.

Thank you for the blessing You've bestowed upon me and grant me humility and kindness as I pay back.

Thomas R Cutrera

July 1

ONE LESSON I HAVE LEARNED IN MY LIFE IS...

Summers are hot in Arizona. As obvious as that sounds, by mid-July, nothing stops me from complaining. By then, I have completely forgot-ten about the incredible winter and fabulous spring we enjoyed. All I know is that I am hot. And I let everyone know about it.

In my head I am aware that this side of heaven nothing is perfect. Lights turn red. Traffic backs up. Food gets cold. And, things go wrong. And yet, no matter how much I complain, all these things keep happening. By July 1, I know one thing for sure. I need more patience.

PRAYER FOR THE BLESSING OF THE DAY...

Lord God, help me to accept the imperfections of life. Help me to really understand that the world does not revolve around me or my comfort. Help me to enjoy life rather than curse it because it doesn't always go my way. Let the inconveniences of life help me to long for Heaven instead of whining and ruining the day for those around me.

Fr. Dale

July 2

ONE LESSON I HAVE LEARNED IN MY LIFE IS...

Everyone handles change differently. Some folks love change. Some fight it. I like it. In fact, I move my office furniture and home furniture around for no reason at all. Somehow it seems to give me a different perspective on life. Of course bigger changes, like a job, a divorce, a death, a move, are a lot more stressful. But every change offers new opportunities as well as difficulties. As long as we are alive, we need to be flexible and recognize that change is a part of life.

PRAYER FOR THE BLESSING OF THE DAY...

Heavenly Father, help me to change. Open my heart to Your Spirit so that I can become more like Your Son, Jesus. AMEN.

Fr. Dale

July 3

ONE LESSON I HAVE LEARNED IN MY LIFE IS...

All of my planning and trying to figure out the answers to my difficulties are futile. God has the answers. All He asks it that I invite Him into my thoughts, my plans, and my figuring. He always steps in and gives me His wisdom.

[Proverbs 3:5-12, The Message (MSG)]
Trust God from the bottom of your heart;
    Don't try to figure out everything on your own.
Listen for God's voice in everything you do, everywhere you go;
    He's the one who will keep you on track.
Don't assume that you know it all.
    Run to God! Run from evil!
Your body will glow with health,
    Your very bones will vibrate with life!
Honor God with everything you own;
    Give him the first and the best.
Your barns will burst,
    Your wine vats will brim over.
But don't dear friend, resent God's discipline;
    don't sulk under his loving correction.
It's the child he loves that God corrects;
    a father's delight is behind all this.

PRAYER FOR THE BLESSING OF THE DAY…

Thank you, Lord, for the unconditional love and wisdom You so abundantly pour out on me. Your wisdom makes my rough words smooth. Lord, be with me today. Give me Your wisdom. AMEN.

Carol Taylor

July 4

ONE LESSON I HAVE LEARNED IN MY LIFE IS…

This day we remember the freedoms our forefathers fought for and we represent as Americans; they can change dramatically when we take God out of the equation. When man makes laws and rules, we eventually become enslaved and bound by those laws. We lose the freedoms God gives us.

PRAYER FOR THE BLESSING OF THE DAY…

God, we come into Your presence to be cleansed of our attachment to the things of the world that keep us in captivity. Your son Jesus was tempted by Satan, master of the world, yet He rejected those temptations and fulfilled His purpose, to save mankind. Thank You for that power and promise to overcome the world. AMEN.

(Proverbs 2:7)

"He holds victory in store for the upright, he is the shield to those whose walk is blameless, for he guards the course of the just and protects the way of his faithful ones."

John & Sandie Null

July 5

ONE LESSON I HAVE LEARNED IN MY LIFE IS...

When I hit the brick walls of my life, God is waiting patiently for me to cry, "HELP, I can't find my way through all of this. I am lost and I can't figure this out."

When I cry to God, He hears my cry. He answers my cry. He wants me to cry out and submit to Him. He is always there. He always provides His way.

[Jeremiah 33:3; King James Version (KJV)]

Call unto me, and I will answer thee, and show thee great and mighty things, which thou knowest not.

PRAYER FOR THE BLESSING OF THE DAY...

Thank you, Lord. You are always there, just waiting for my cry for help. Lord, forgive me for my proud heart, forgive me for my pride. Thank you, Lord for Your faithfulness to me. AMEN.

Carol Taylor

July 6

ONE LESSON I HAVE LEARNED IN MY LIFE IS...

How beautiful is the SILENCE! I first experienced the silence when hiking down into the Grand Canyon. Going beneath the rim, even 200 feet, can give the hiker that experience. It is awesome. And then knowing that the exposed rock is billions of years old, one experiences the origins of the earth before mankind. If all of time is a 24-hour clock, mankind only appeared in the last few minutes. And THAT is awesome.

The silence can also be reached in the art of meditation. Learning to shut off the conscious voices blabbering in my mind, I can reach the silence. It is there that I sing, "Be still, and know that I am (your) God." (Psalm 46:10)

PRAYER FOR THE BLESSING OF THE DAY...

Dear Lord, please help me to reach the silence, to listen, to understand Your plan for my soul.

For there is where I experience "the peace that passes all understanding." (Philippians 4:7).

Jean Bruno

July 7

ONE LESSON I HAVE LEARNED IN MY LIFE IS...

Never give up on reconciliation. After all the bad stuff happened in my life, I didn't speak to someone for a decade! This "someone" was like a brother to me, one of the closest people I had in my inner circle. I would have bet my life this person would be at my side, even at my death bed (many years from now). But, hurts happen. And in this case, they did. And it prevented us from speaking for more than 10 years. To say it hurt would be an understatement.

Then we talked. He didn't want to talk about the past -- just the future. That was fine with me. The miracle was WE TALKED. I prayed hard this would happen. And it finally did.

I'm still not sure exactly how it happened. But, I know, it was the power of the Holy Spirit. The Spirit can move even the hardest hearts.

PRAYER FOR THE BLESSING OF THE DAY...

Thank you, Lord, for answered prayers. Remind me, when I don't feel like praying, that prayer does matter. AMEN.

Fr. Dale

July 8

ONE LESSON I HAVE LEARNED IN MY LIFE IS...

Not to take myself too seriously. Sometimes, I simply need to laugh at myself. And I should never be surprised when someone else laughs at me, either. I am sure God cherishes all of us.

Spiritual writer Brennan Manning wrote one of the best quotes I have ever read. He said, "When a man or a woman is truly honest, it is virtually impossible to insult them personally."

Those are strong words, but they are true. When we are humble about ourselves, we know our own weaknesses, sinfulness, and our own imperfection. After many years I am learning it is okay to be honest about them.

PRAYER FOR THE BLESSING OF THE DAY...

(Psalm 139)

"You have searched me, Lord,
    and You know me.
You know when I sit and when I rise;
    You perceive my thoughts from afar.
You discern my going out and my lying down;
    You are familiar with all my ways."

Fr. Dale

July 9

ONE LESSON I HAVE LEARNED IN MY LIFE IS...

Not everybody gets to play the drums in the orchestra.

When I was very young, I thought my future contained a lot more percussion than my parents were eager to take on. When I got to an age when I wanted to join the school orchestra, I requested the drums. I was instead directed towards the string section, which is where I ultimately ended up – on the other end of a cello for years and years.

I'd like to say that eventually I returned to my real passion – the drums – and left strings and bows behind me in a cloud of rosin dust. However, I did not. I played the cello quite happily for a very long time, because I loved the entire experience of making music with other people.

Sometimes not getting what you think you want works out anyway.

PRAYER FOR THE BLESSING OF THE DAY...

Lord, we are told "don't settle" when it comes to the things we strive for in life. However, I am asking You to help me learn to settle more than I do. Show me the way to temper my expectations with realism, and to be grateful for the unexpected ways that life can be enriched.

Jody Serey

July 10

ONE LESSON I HAVE LEARNED IN MY LIFE IS...

Life is filled with storms. Storms are sometimes inconvenient, sometimes life giving, and sometimes life changing. After Christmas in 2004, my life was hit by a tsunami. Bizarre and untrue allegations were made against me, and I was removed from my home, my life, and my vocation. After these allegations, the next few years were filled with church and civil leaders publically pleading for allegations to come forward. A year later, 20-year-old misdemeanor charges were filed.

The poet T.S. Elliot says, "No one changes except out of pain." Change is GOOD. Without change there is no growth and no new revelations. It was only when Christ changed at the Transfiguration that the Apostles knew who He is. My changes certainly grew out of my pain -- and the pain of many others that I love.

The word "change" actually comes from the old Latin term meaning to barter or exchange. Perhaps that's what really happens in CHANGING -- we are bartering with God, or with the universe. We are giving something of who we are away and accepting something else in its place. Like any barters, sometimes we win and sometimes we lose. Sometimes it's good, other times, not so good. The bottom line is, if we are ever going to go more deeply into the mystery of God, we have to be open to changing.

PRAYER FOR THE BLESSING OF THE DAY...

Lord, don't let me be filled with fear! May my faith always be stronger than my fear. AMEN.

Fr. Dale

July 11

ONE LESSON I HAVE LEARNED IN MY LIFE IS...

It is important to care for others. The Gospel of Jesus Christ goes contrary to the norms of our culture. As a society, we have become very self-centered. But Jesus teaches us to care for others as deeply as we care for ourselves. Caring for others, however, does not mean becoming co-dependent (you become responsible for what someone else should be doing for themselves). Co-dependency is not about true care for others; it is really about doing things that make you feel good. It is a sick sense of love and care. Genuine care for others is to love another with the heart of Jesus.

PRAYER FOR THE BLESSING OF THE DAY...

In Paul's letters to the Philippians (2:4) we are told, "...do not look out for our own interests, but also for the interests of others." Lord, may I fulfill this teaching of St. Paul today. Please give me the opportunity to love someone else this day. AMEN.

Fr. Dale

July 12

ONE LESSON I HAVE LEARNED IN MY LIFE IS...

Life goes on whether we do or not.

PRAYER FOR THE BLESSING OF THE DAY...

Lord, help me get up, get dressed, and get going. Do not let me lie down when I should rise up. Keep me moving forward, onward, and upward. Help me embrace the challenges of the day and my circumstances with courage, and the confidence that comes from knowing You see me and will not let me fail.

Jody Serey

July 13

ONE LESSON I HAVE LEARNED IN MY LIFE IS...

The world is constantly changing. Technology has provided us with so many gadgets that it's very frustrating trying to keep them all straight. However, it has also given us a significantly different view of places near and far. Certainly quite a change from when I was born (??) years ago today.

Therefore, my goal for the following year is to go with the changes -- maybe not so much with the machines, but with people. I want to be more tolerant of those whose religion and language are strange to me; to understand better the people who have lifestyles different from mine; to be patient with everyone and to be a shining example of God's unconditional love.

PRAYER FOR THE BLESSING OF THE DAY...

Loving God, thank you for the changes around us. Give us the guidance we need to accept these changes with open minds and hearts. In Jesus' name we pray. AMEN.

(Luke 6:37-38)

Betty Clewell

July 14

ONE LESSON I HAVE LEARNED IN MY LIFE IS...

Good friends are a gift from God. Good friends know who we are and they love us for who we are. They walk with us though the highs and lows of life. They are God's hands in our lives; they are His support, and they are His encouragement for us. They are the hugs He sends to show us how very much He loves us. God has used my friends to get me through some very bumpy parts of life and my friends have helped me celebrate the mountaintop experiences and give glory to Him. I give Him thanks and praise for the friends that He has blessed me with in my life. I pray He uses me the same way in their lives.

PRAYER FOR THE BLESSING OF THE DAY...

Dear Lord, I give You thanks and praise for the blessing of friendship in my life. I thank You for showing the depth of the love You have for me through my friends. They've helped me discover more about You in my life. I thank You for the blessings and gifts they are to me and I pray that You use me to show them more of You and to help them feel the love You have for them. In Jesus' name I pray. AMEN.

Debbie Smith

July 15

ONE LESSON I HAVE LEARNED IN MY LIFE IS...

The United States of America does not have a justice system. We have a legal system. There is a big difference. Justice is about everything being in right order, ethical, and fair. Legal simply means according to the law and the process our society has set up.

As Christians, however, we know that true justice belongs to God. He will right all wrongs one day and our job is simply to allow Him to act justly. We can trust, too, that He will always mix in mercy along with justice.

We should always work for justice in this world. We cannot ignore injustice. But we also know that this life is imperfect. God, in the long run will bring perfect justice.

PRAYER FOR THE BLESSING OF THE DAY...

Lord, help me to seek justice for those who cannot defend themselves. But help me also to know, that You are the God of true justice. As Psalm 89 (vs14) says, "Your kingdom is ruled by justice, with love and faithfulness leading the way."

Fr. Dale

July 16

ONE LESSON I HAVE LEARNED IN MY LIFE IS...

"It will all change." Those are the words that Mother Teresa spoke to me when I commented on the cheering crowd and the crush of people wanting to put money and checks into her hands.

"It will all change." Her words shocked me, and I paused briefly as they sank in. But I knew she was right. The cheers would stop. Silence would return. And she would be gone someday.

Nothing – good or bad – lasts forever. Only the works and words of love that we offer each other can continue without decay.

PRAYER FOR THE BLESSING OF THE DAY...

Lord, in an inconstant world, let me turn to You for what is everlasting, unchanging, and unaffected by the tide of public opinion and human folly. Let me feel Your goodness, even when all seems to be defiled. Remind me to hope, despite the doubt that tries to claim me.

Jody Serey

July 17

ONE LESSON I HAVE LEARNED IN MY LIFE IS...

Evil is present in our world. Evil tends not to come to us in a two-horned devil, but rather in chaos, narcissism, and the need that others have to control and bully. Evil comes to us in terrorism, gangs, and lies. Albert Einstein said "The world is a dangerous place to live, not because of the people who are evil, but because of the people who don't do anything about it."

None of us wants to focus on evil. But we cannot hide from it, either. We must, as individuals, and as a nation, be willing to stand up for the truth and confront evil, no matter how it comes to us.

The good news is (1 John 4:4) that "the Spirit who lives in you is greater than the Spirit who lives in the world." Jesus showed His power over the evil spirits in scripture. Evil is real. But, it is powerless in the presence of TRUTH.

PRAYER FOR THE BLESSING OF THE DAY...

Lord, end the chaos and confusion of our world. Please put an end to terrorism, selfishness, and greed. Help us all to live in Your Spirit. AMEN.

Fr. Dale

July 18

ONE LESSON I HAVE LEARNED IN MY LIFE IS...

Communal praise and worship evolve, mature within each individual AND within each assembly, each community.

In the beginning, I accepted that salvation would happen after I learned to follow all the rules and commandments. If I did what was prescribed, what was being taught, I'd get into heaven. Because that was my "goal," I decided to try to play by the rules. I could do it, with God's help.

I remember being surprised when this concept was disparaged as "Jacob's Ladder." Then, beginning with Vatican II, I found myself on a journey to refocus, from individualized efforts into communal activity, described as "Sarah's Circle."

It's been a radical enlightenment, an evolutionary revolution, to come to the understanding of "We're in this together!" I began to notice prayers and songs that used plural rather than singular pronouns: "Find Us Ready," "We Have Set Our Hearts For The Way," "Hear Us, O Lord," and "We Believe." It's now encouraging to be operating in this environment.

PRAYER FOR THE BLESSING OF THE DAY...

Let's meditate on all areas of our communal life together. Our lamentations, our rejoicings, our gratitude, love, our petitions, our hope, our forgiveness. Our community, work, charity, our support, compassion, and service. In your prayer, you are encouraged to continue this litany.

Terry J Bolduc

July 19

ONE LESSON I HAVE LEARNED IN MY LIFE IS...

A house is a structure. A home is where memories are made, and who and what you love reside.

PRAYER FOR THE BLESSING OF THE DAY...

Lord, bless my house that it may be a sanctuary for all things that enter my door. May evil find no corner to lurk in, and may anger and violence find nothing here to cling to. Let my family remember the stories we told and the laughter that we would not suppress, even when times were hard and our hearts were broken. And someday when our voices no longer fill these rooms, let the ones who follow after us know that as for me and my house, we served You, our Lord.

Jody Serey

July 20

ONE LESSON I HAVE LEARNED IN MY LIFE IS...

The message of Jesus Christ is difficult to live. He calls us to love our enemies, turn the other cheek, and to forgive seven times seventy times. It sounds overwhelming! And in the Beatitudes (Matthew 5:3-11), He calls us to have an amazing love which calls us to hunger and thirst for justice.

Jesus would not call us to these exceptional things without giving us the help we need. He promised and delivered the Holy Spirit to us. The Spirit brings gifts of Wisdom, Knowledge, Counsel, Piety, Fortitude, Understanding and Fear of the Lord. These gifts give us the ability and the desire to "build up the body of Christ" by following the teachings of Christ.

The Holy Spirit is a person, not a thing. The Holy Spirit is God. So, it is the God who dwells within us that helps us to become more Godly people. We are not left on our own to follow Christ. We have incredible help.

PRAYER FOR THE BLESSING OF THE DAY...

Come, Holy Spirit! Fill the hearts of Your faithful. Enkindle in us, the fire of Your love. AMEN.

Fr. Dale

July 21

ONE LESSON I HAVE LEARNED IN MY LIFE IS...

God, my mommy, daddy, grandparents, aunts, uncles, and cousins all love me.

PRAYER FOR THE BLESSING OF THE DAY...

Lord, as I lay down to sleep, have Your angels watch over me and my family.

Mackenzie Siegel

July 22

ONE LESSON I HAVE LEARNED IN MY LIFE IS...

The worse I look, the more people I will run into when I try to sneak into the grocery store unobserved to buy dog food and a large pack of something embarassing. One old sweatshirt with kittens on it almost guarantees a reunion with somebody from my past.

PRAYER FOR THE BLESSING OF THE DAY...

Lord, let me care a lot less about what people think, and more about how they feel. Help me find ways to focus on the one standing before me. Let me pay attention to what is being said, and ignore my own anxiousness about creating a good impression.

Jody Serey

July 23

ONE LESSON I HAVE LEARNED IN MY LIFE IS...

I need to laugh more. I think I take stuff way too seriously. Believe me, I know, there is a lot of pain and suffering in the world. But, I also know there are a lot of funny people (they may not know it) and funny situations.

I remember giving a very strong message on pro-life at the teen service one Sunday night. I was passionately pacing across the sanctuary. As I ended, I kicked a glass of water by accident and it shattered. Our musician, Matt Maher, announced, "Wow, FD, I knew you were pro-life, but I never expected us to witness your water breaking." VERY funny. I think God laughed, too.

PRAYER FOR THE BLESSING OF THE DAY...

Father, in the book of Ecclesiastes, Your word says, "There is a time to be born and a time, a time to plant and a time to uproot, a time to kill, a time to heal, a time to tear down, and a time to build, a time to weep and a time to laugh."

May I find time to laugh today. AMEN.

Fr. Dale

July 24

ONE LESSON I HAVE LEARNED IN MY LIFE IS...

When I forgive someone it allows me to let go of the negative feelings that I have been harboring for the one who hurt or wronged me. I can move on with my life and have a sense of peacefulness that I didn't have when I was angry and holding a grudge. I came to the realization that the only one I'm hurting by holding a grudge is me! When I think about certain instances that made me angry with someone, it would just cause the anger to surface again and the more I would dwell on it the more upset I would get. It's a vicious cycle that I needed to break for my own good. So I decided to pray for healing for them as well as for me. After all, we are both sinners and we are both children of God. We each have our weaknesses and our strengths and by letting them continue to affect my life in a negative way (by replaying past events in my mind) I'm giving them power over me and allowing them to continue hurting me (whether they even know it or not). So when I turn this around and look at them as the weak one who needs help, I can forgive them and pray that they get the help that they need.

PRAYER FOR THE BLESSING OF THE DAY...

Lord, help me to forgive as You forgive and to not judge others on their actions. Help me to see others as You see them and feel the love that You feel for each and every one of us. Bless us, Lord, with peace in our hearts so that we may see You in the faces of others. Guide us in Your ways, Lord, and bring us all closer to You. I ask these things in Jesus' name. AMEN.

Maureen Broudy

July 25

ONE LESSON I HAVE LEARNED IN MY LIFE IS...

My view of prayer keeps changing. As a kid, it was learning words to say to God. As an adult, it became learning to talk to God in my own words. Now it means listening to God.

The great spiritual writer Henri Nouwen says, "To pray means to open your hands before God. It means slowly relaxing the tension which squeezes your hands together and accepting your existence with an increasing readiness, not as a possession to defend, but as a gift to receive" (from "With Open Hands").

I know God has gifts for all of us. We need to open our hands and our hearts need to receive them.

PRAYER FOR THE BLESSING OF THE DAY...

(Prayer by Henri Nouwen)

"Dear God,
      I do not know where You are leading me.
      I do not even know what my next day,
      my next week, or my next year will look like.
      As I try to keep my hands open,
      I trust that You will put Your hand in mine
      and bring me home.
      Thank you, God, for Your love.
      Thank you. AMEN."

Fr. Dale

July 26

ONE LESSON I HAVE LEARNED IN MY LIFE IS...

Sometimes we have to face our fears. When I was nine or ten I had a paper route in my neighborhood. I will never forget 7429 Villa Way. It was a very long street and only had one street light on it. Worse yet, it was one filled with barking dogs. During the week, the paper was delivered in the afternoon, so I could see what was in front of me, and avoid the DOGS!!!! However, Sunday morning the paper was delivered in the morning, before the sun came up. I was so fearful of that street. Then it happened -- I was face to face with a black German shepherd. In a shear moment of panic, I let out a scream of fear for my life. One by one the lights on the porches came on, and people came out to see what was wrong. The owner of the dog came up and introduced me to Duchess, a dog that liked to get the morning paper. My fear was over knowing now what was brought to light.

All too often we let our emotions get the best of us. We over-think things and let fear rule our lives. Jesus reminds us that we are called to bring things to the light. In a simple cry for help, we could be surrounded by His mercy and love.

Today, let us face our fears, and cry out to GOD for His protection and love -- knowing when we bring something to light we bring it to GOD.

(Isaiah 41:10)

"Do not fear, for I am with you always."

PRAYER FOR THE BLESSING OF THE DAY...

Heavenly Father, give me the courage today to face my fears. Let me be mindful that when I cry out to You in prayer, that You are there for me, and surrounding me with the light of Your love. May I today not focus on fear, but on Your love. AMEN.

Mark Dippre

July 27

ONE LESSON I HAVE LEARNED IN MY LIFE IS...

Being a compassionate person is not easy. It is easy to become hardhearted and uncaring. After all, every one of us has been hurt. But to choose compassion -- that is, to feel with someone else -- is a choice that we can make.

The bible is clear that God is compassionate with us. In return, He teaches us to have compassion with one another. In 1 Peter 3:8, God says, "Finally, all of you should be of one mind. Sympathize with each other. Love each other as brothers and sisters. Be tenderhearted, and keep a humble attitude."

It is easier to not care. But, it is also ungodly. The world doesn't need any more of that!

PRAYER FOR THE BLESSING OF THE DAY...

Lord, soften my heart today. Let me listen and care for someone else today. Allow me to enter someone else's world just as You have entered mine. Allow me Lord, to love someone today with Your heart instead of mine. AMEN.

Fr. Dale

July 28

ONE LESSON I HAVE LEARNED IN MY LIFE IS...

Cotton is not the fabric of our lives. I know that is what the cotton industry says in the advertising. But, it doesn't mean it's true. Actually, I believe that LOVE is the fabric of our lives. Love is what weaves meaning and purpose into our being. Love is what adds texture to the tasks we do and the events we are involved in. And when all is said and done, love is the only thing that survives this life and carries on to eternity. Cotton is a great thing to wear on a hot day, but love is all that really matters. I need to let love truly be the center of my life.

PRAYER FOR THE BLESSING OF THE DAY...

Thank you, Father, for the gift of Your Love. Please allow me to be an instrument of Your Love for others. Let my whole life be centered in Love.

Fr. Dale

July 29

ONE LESSON I HAVE LEARNED IN MY LIFE IS...

I am very sensitive about my eyes. I hate going to the eye doctor or even putting drops in my eyes. Because of that, I am extremely compassionate when I see someone who is blind or seeing impaired. I always wonder if they have always been blind or if something happened along life's way.

Jesus was evidently compassionate to the physically blind. He put mud on the eyes of the man born blind and healed him. (John 9:1-12) He was not so compassionate with the spiritually blind and self-righteous. Jesus said to them, "If you were blind, you would not have sin. But, you say 'we see', and your sin remains."

PRAYER FOR THE BLESSING OF THE DAY...

Jesus said, "I am the light of the world." Lord Jesus, I pray that I may see You as You are, the real light for all people. Help me, Jesus, to fill the darkness in my heart with the light of Your love. AMEN.

Fr. Dale

July 30

ONE LESSON I HAVE LEARNED IN MY LIFE IS...

If you want the apple, you have to factor in the possibility of a worm. And he isn't going to be happy about your plans for the apple.

PRAYER FOR THE BLESSING OF THE DAY...

Lord, please help me remember that everything I do impacts something or somebody. Don't let me become immune to the discomfort of others at my hands, even when it is unavoidable.

Jody Serey

July 31

ONE LESSON I HAVE LEARNED IN MY LIFE IS...

When the stakes are highest, always bet on red.

Now I'm not talking about gambling here, I'm talking about the blood of Jesus. When Jesus died on the cross, He paid the penalty for our sin, setting us free from the bondage that came with it. With that action came a promise: If we choose to accept Him as our Savior, He would never leave us or forsake us. He has our backs no matter what. I've seen God come through for me on numerous occasions, but the one that stands out the most was when I found myself stranded in an airport in Germany. I had been on my way to the United States after graduating from high school from Budapest, Hungary, where I had lived as a missionary for 10 years. I was traveling with my sister and her boy-friend, so I wasn't completely alone, but this was the first time I had traveled without real adult supervision. Needless to say, I was anxious. We landed in Frankfurt and had to rush to the check-in counter for our next flight. But when we got there, they had already closed for the night. So we found a spot to rest and enjoy our luxurious 14-hour over-night stay in the airport. The next morning, exhausted, we headed over to the check in counter. When we got to the front of the line, we were told that our carry-on luggage was too big and we would have to pay 50 euros each to check them, or we would not be allowed on the flight. We had no idea what to do. We had no money, no way of contacting my parents, and no way to get home. Hours went by, and our flight time was getting closer and closer. We tried talking to the employees. They sent us from desk to desk and no one could help us. Finally, I remembered God's promise. I prayed. I instantly felt a peace wash over me, and I walked up to the counter again. This time, they called a manager who was asleep at home, waking him up to tell him about our situation. The manager decided to pay for our bags to be checked, so that we could get home! When we got on our plane, I sat there, amazed at how incredible God is that He was there for us! Whenever situations arise that push my limits, I have learned to lean back and rest in the arms of Jesus and let Him see me through the storm. When we bet on Jesus, we never lose.

PRAYER FOR THE BLESSING OF THE DAY...

God, thank you for being with me and guiding me throughout all of my trials. Help me to trust You today, that whatever happens I will know that You have my back. Thank you for loving me and for caring about every aspect of my life. In Your name, I pray. AMEN.

David Person

August 1

ONE LESSON I HAVE LEARNED IN MY LIFE IS...

True compassion is a strength, not a weakness. The word itself comes from Latin and it means "to suffer with." Compassion allows us to feel grief with someone who loses a parent, child, or spouse. Compassion allows us to feel with a hungry or sick child. It also moves us to forgive someone who has hurt us or who has hurt those we love.

PRAYER FOR THE BLESSING OF THE DAY...

Lord, in the busy-ness of our own lives, help us to be able to respond to those who are in pain. Be with those whose hearts are hurting and broken. Help us to go deeper into Your heart of compassion and healing.

Fr. Dale

August 2

ONE LESSON I HAVE LEARNED IN MY LIFE IS...

Life changes quickly. Recently, my 18 year old nephew collapsed on the football field. He basically had a heart attack caused by an undetected defect in the heart present since birth. No one knew it was there. Praise God the fire department saved his life. No one, especially an 18 year old young man, expects life to change that quickly.

Jesus tells us in scripture that we must live prepared. He uses the symbol of keeping our torches lit as a reminder that we must always expect the unexpected. He doesn't ask us to be fearful or "crazy" cautious. He simply reminds us to check our oil, to be on guard, to be vigilant.

My mother's house was broken in to. We didn't have an alarm on the house. We do now. We should have been more prepared! So today, I need to evaluate my readiness. Readiness for what? That's the million dollar question. I need to be ready for whatever comes my way.

PRAYER FOR THE BLESSING OF THE DAY...

(Matthew 25:13)

"Keep awake therefore, for you know neither the day nor the hour." Lord, for whatever comes my way today, may I be prepared and grateful. AMEN.

Fr. Dale

August 3

ONE LESSON I HAVE LEARNED IN MY LIFE IS...

We have to care for our souls. In his book Soul Keeping, John Ortberg says, "For the soul to be well, it needs to be with God." That means we need to make a conscious choice for our soul to be aware of God. Prayer helps our souls. Worship helps our souls. Quiet helps our souls. Ortberg explains, "This God – the God of the Bible – is a God who wants to 'be with'. Our souls were made to walk with God. Each day we need to remind ourselves that God is walking the journey with us. And if we don't stop Him, He will nourish our souls."

PRAYER FOR THE BLESSING OF THE DAY...

Father, I give You my heart, my soul, and my very being. Nourish my soul today with Your grace. Let me be aware of Your presence each moment of my day. I know You walk with me Jesus, help me to walk with You. AMEN.

Fr. Dale

August 4

ONE LESSON I HAVE LEARNED IN MY LIFE IS...

We are all in charge of our own happiness. It's much easier to blame someone else if my life is unhappy. But the truth is I have to make the choices in my life to create that happiness. The choice to be happy starts with the acknowledgement that God wills my happiness -- not my misery. Our God loves us and desires good for us. And even though events happen that create pain for us, we can still choose to do things that help us to find peace inside us. As a popular Christian song says, we can praise God "even in these storms."

PRAYER FOR THE BLESSING OF THE DAY...

(John 14:25-27)

"I have said these things to you while I am still with you. But the Advocate, the Holy Spirit, whom the Father will send in my name, will teach you everything, and remind you of all that I have said to you.

Peace I leave with you; my peace I give to you. I do not give to you as the world gives. Do not let your hearts be troubled, and do not let them be afraid."

Fr. Dale

August 5

ONE LESSON I HAVE LEARNED IN MY LIFE IS...

The more expensive the outfit the grandparents send, the faster the baby outgrows it.

PRAYER FOR THE BLESSING OF THE DAY...

Lord, help me always honor the intent of another's kind gesture. Let me feel gratitude for the love symbolized by the gift, and never find fault with the object being given. Let me truly be grateful for the people who claim me as their own, and who celebrate who and what I love.

Jody Serey

August 6

ONE LESSON I HAVE LEARNED IN MY LIFE IS...

Life is short and you don't know when your time to go is. Are you living it the way you are intended? Five years ago I was critically ill with sepsis. I went into a medical coma. My family and friends were at my bedside in the intensive care unit daily for a month. I had a near death experience and saw them praying over me. I was given another chance in life and was told my purpose wasn't complete. Those words stayed clear and forefront in my mind. I daily tried to understand the words. At first I searched to fulfill my own needs. Something was drawing me to seek more. I wanted something deeper and more meaningful. I prayed and continue to pray for understanding daily. I see and feel myself changing. My relationship with the Lord has become more intimate. I spend time with the Lord daily, and I don't know where the journey of life takes me this day, but I know I'm loved and need to spread that love to others.

PRAYER FOR THE BLESSING OF THE DAY...

I have been crucified with Christ. It is no longer I who live, but Christ who lives in me. And the life I now live in the flesh I live by faith in the Son of God who loved me and gave himself for me. (Galatians 2:20)

But God, being rich in mercy, because of the great love with which he loved us, even when we were dead in our trespasses, made us alive together with Christ – by grace you have been saved. (Ephesians 2:4-5)

Beloved, let us love one another, for love is from God, and whoever loves has been born of God and knows God. Anyone who does not love does not know God, because God is Love.

(1 John 4:7-8)

Kathy L. Davis

August 7

ONE LESSON I HAVE LEARNED IN MY LIFE IS...

Never to hold yourself higher up than you need to. If you expect too much from yourself, you will always fail. I have learned that it is ok to strive as far as you can make it, but nothing more. If you try your hardest, that is all anyone can ask of you. But if you raise the bar too high, you will always be let down.

PRAYER FOR THE BLESSING OF THE DAY...

Lord, help me try my best and be my best today. AMEN.

Peter Rehm-Gerdes

August 8

ONE LESSON I HAVE LEARNED IN MY LIFE IS...

Stuff happens. Things occur that you can't control -- so you just need to accept them and take the next steps.

PRAYER FOR THE BLESSING OF THE DAY...

God, help me grow up loving You.

Kennedy Broderson

August 9

ONE LESSON I HAVE LEARNED IN MY LIFE IS...

That not everything that looks holy, is holy. Jesus encountered the same thing with the Pharisees. They wanted everyone to see them as pure, but, on the inside, they were full of sin.

I've often wondered if true holiness starts on the inside and then changes the outside behavior, or if the right behavior on the outside eventually works its way in to change a person's heart. I guess God can work however He chooses to work. But, I do know this -- real holiness has to be authentic. Because when God is fully received, God changes our hearts, our feelings, our thoughts, and our behaviors. I want to be AUTHENTICALLY holy!

PRAYER FOR THE BLESSING OF THE DAY...

Lord Jesus Christ, I declare You to be our Lord and Savior. I want to please You with every part of my life. I ask You to give me the grace and strength to be authentically holy! AMEN.

Fr. Dale

August 10

ONE LESSON I HAVE LEARNED IN MY LIFE IS...

The best way to pray is with our hands open. Why? There are two reasons. First, because that is how Christians prayed in the early days. It showed they were open and waiting for the second coming of Jesus Christ. The second reason, I believe, is that it shows we are totally open to the Holy Spirit. As we know, prayer should never come from just us. True prayer is the Holy Spirit praying in us and through us. The most beautiful and meaningful prayer is the Spirit praising Jesus and praising our Heavenly Father, through our bodies and our words.

Pray today, with an open heart. And try, as you pray, to open your hands. Lift your hands to the Lord, and let the Spirit take over.

PRAYER FOR THE BLESSING OF THE DAY...

Come Holy Spirit. Fill the hearts of Your faithful. And enkindle in me the fire of Your love. AMEN.

Fr. Dale

August 11

ONE LESSON I HAVE LEARNED IN MY LIFE IS...

I am no St. Paul. I know he loved to preach, and so do I. And, I know he loved being a pastor, and so do I. But, Paul was a man totally on fire. And for me, although that is my desire, it is not always my reality.

One of the things I have learned about myself is that I can allow things to distract me. St. Paul seemed like he never did. Paul writes with passion and faith even when he is in prison. Whether it was a shipwreck, rejection, prison, or hunger -- Paul kept his passion for Jesus. I pray I can do the same.

PRAYER FOR THE BLESSING OF THE DAY...

St. Paul said (Philippians 4:12), "I know what it is to have little, and I know what it is to have plenty. In any and all circumstances, I have learned the secret of being well fed and of going hungry, of having plenty and of being in need."

Lord, teach me, no matter what, to stay focused on You.

Fr. Dale

August 12

ONE LESSON I HAVE LEARNED IN MY LIFE IS...

To always keep my eyes, mind and heart open to the presence, grace, blessings and healing of God in my life, every moment of every day. We give thanks and praise to God in good times for the many blessings and gifts He bestows upon us. It can be difficult, for even devout followers of Christ, to give thanks and praise to God in our trying and most difficult times, for it is those dark and desperate challenges in life's journey that bring us closer to Him. When we grow closer to God, we gain a clear and focused understanding and knowledge of His plan for our lives, and experience that there is so much to learn and share from adversity and the speed bumps we incur along our journey.

PRAYER FOR THE BLESSING OF THE DAY...

Lord, thank You for giving me everything I need to walk in faith and overcome what the enemy throws at me. Whatever obstacles stand in my way today, You are greater. Thank you for the favor You have given me to keep rising up and overcoming. I will live joyfully because You walk with me. AMEN.

Elizabeth James

August 13

ONE LESSON I HAVE LEARNED IN MY LIFE IS...

We are sometimes try to hide our greatest pain from others. Perhaps our precious child died...we were raped or tortured...we have an invisible disability...we are transsexual...we accidentally killed another human being...we suffer addiction or mental illness...our corporation goes bankrupt through no fault of our own...we are harshly or wrongly judged and lose most of our friends...

We want to hide from the world -- but God eventually reveals to us our humiliation and weakness is actually our gift to others. If we allow God to use us, God graces us with His love, His empathy and compassion for others in our or a similar situation. God will use us to befriend and help others if we are brave and let him.

PRAYER FOR THE BLESSING OF THE DAY...

(Romans 8:28; 35) "We are assured and know that [God being a partner in their labor] all things work together and are [fitting into a plan] for good to and for those who love God and are called according to [His] design and purposes."

Anonymous

August 14

ONE LESSON I HAVE LEARNED IN MY LIFE IS...

I should pray the psalms more often! They are spectacular prayers that cover every human emotion and human situation. The psalms praise

God in eloquent ways. The psalms also cry to God for mercy and help. Over the past 3,000 years, Christians and Jews have found no better way to pray than to use the words of the psalms. Jesus prayed them often as well. If Jesus himself used them to honor God -- I would be wise to do the same!

PRAYER FOR THE BLESSING OF THE DAY...

(Psalm 9, Verses 1-2)

"I will give thanks to the Lord with my whole heart;

I will tell of all Your wonderful deeds.

I will be glad and exalt in You;

I will sing praise to Your name, most High."

Fr. Dale

August 15

ONE LESSON I HAVE LEARNED IN MY LIFE IS...

That sometimes scripture seems to give mixed messages. On the one hand, we are supposed to be humble and not prideful. And on the other hand, I was just reading in scripture (Mark 4:21-22) not to hide our light under a bushel basket. So, which is it?

The answer is to go deeper into the meaning of what the Word is saying. If we have gifts, talents, blessings, insights or wisdom we should always share them. God doesn't give us these gifts to keep to ourselves, but rather to light our world. However, when the spotlight turns on us, that's when we are called to move out of the way and let God be glorified. That's when we realize and publically say, "It's not me, it is God simply using me."

We need to go light our world. There's plenty of darkness out there. But in the end, it is the light of Jesus Christ that actually brightens the hearts and souls of people.

PRAYER FOR THE BLESSING OF THE DAY...

(John 1:3-5)

"All things came into being through Him, and without Him not one thing came into being. What has come into being in Him was life, and the life was the light of all people. The light shines in the darkness, and the darkness did not overcome it."

Lord, let me reflect the light of Your love. AMEN.

Fr. Dale

August 16

ONE LESSON I HAVE LEARNED IN MY LIFE IS...

After what seemed such long time, I finally married the man of my dreams on August 15th. On the morning of August 16th, I awoke a different person.

Had I changed overnight? Did I look different? Did act differently? No to each of these questions. But yet I was different. I could feel it in every ounce of my being. What had changed?

The simple act of our marriage ceremony the night before had changed who I was. I was now a legal, moral and intrinsic emotional part of another human being. I was a wife with all of the responsibilities of being a wife. I had the potential of becoming a mother, and eventually becoming a grandmother.

Naively I had uttered my positive responses to all my marriage vows and had agreed to enter into a lifetime that would change me forever. I did become a wife, I did become a mother, and I did become a grandmother and even a great and a great-great grandmother. Yes, I became a different person -- yet in many ways I am still the same basic person God created.

[1 Corinthians 13:6-8(NIV)]

"Love does not delight in evil but rejoices with the truth. It always protects, always trusts, always hopes, and always perseveres. Love never fails."

Has it been easy? Of course not. Has it been worth it all? Absolutely, yes!

PRAYER FOR THE BLESSING OF THE DAY...

Lord, thank you for being part of my marriage and making it worth-while. Thank you for all the easy and hard lessons You have taught me through all of those times. Thank you Lord that You have now taken my mate to Glory to spend eternity with You. I so look forward to when it is my time to go Home to be with You in heaven.

Carol Taylor

August 17

ONE LESSON I HAVE LEARNED IN MY LIFE IS...

No one is perfect! We all have our faults and weaknesses. But, the scripture passage "Be perfect; therefore, as your Heavenly Father is perfect" haunts me. (Matthew 5:48)

Do we need to keep striving to be as perfect as God?

Scripture scholars clarify the teaching in Matthew. Jesus is calling us to perfection in LOVE of our enemies (see Matthew 5:43-47). We should strive to imitate God in our love for others.

Having said that, the scriptures never tell us that God's love for us is based upon our perfection. God's love is unconditional -- even when we fail. And though we always strive to do our best, God does not base His love on our performance, but on His perfection in love.

PRAYER FOR THE BLESSING OF THE DAY...

Father, help me to accept my weaknesses as well as the weaknesses and failings of others. Let me become more perfect in loving You and others.

Fr. Dale

August 18

ONE LESSON I HAVE LEARNED IN MY LIFE IS...

Shame is a useless emotion. Shame can come from within ourselves when we feel we have not lived up to our standards. And shame can come from the outside when others feel we have not lived up to their standards. Either way, shame is a negative emotion that rarely motivates someone to make a positive change.

Jesus dealt with shame in the New Testament. When the woman was caught in adultery, the people of the town shamed her and wanted to stone her to death. But Jesus forgave her, raised her eyes from the ground, and sent those who shamed her away. If Jesus rejects shame, we should as well.

PRAYER FOR THE BLESSING OF THE DAY…

(Psalm 34:4-5)

"I sought the Lord, and He answered me, and delivered me from all my fears. Those who look to him are radiant, and their faces shall never be ashamed."

Fr. Dale.

August 19

ONE LESSON I HAVE LEARNED IN MY LIFE IS…

When I try to do things my way, it only leads to disaster one way or another. But, when I ask God to take the reins in a situation and truly trust that He knows best, I see incredible things as a result -- many times more than I imagined!

PRAYER FOR THE BLESSING OF THE DAY…

Lord, continue to lead me and guide me every step of the way in times of struggle and sadness, and times of content and joy. I put my complete trust in You, Abba Father! AMEN.

Kaitlyn Klinzing

August 20

ONE LESSON I HAVE LEARNED IN MY LIFE IS…

God is in charge, if you get out of His way. Well, God is in charge always, but many times we make it more difficult for Him to accomplish His will. We wring our hands and fuss; we take pills; we rant and rave; and maybe, as a last resort, we say a prayer. God should be our first resort in every situation. God is here! And, He knows our every need.

He is waiting for us to invite him in.

PRAYER FOR THE BLESSING OF THE DAY...

God, we love You. And we know You love us. Lead us as we confide in You, first.

Nancy Danielson

August 21

ONE LESSON I HAVE LEARNED IN MY LIFE IS...

Grandchildren are a blessing. They bring a special joy to our lives. As they grow, their exploration and activities can brighten and reignite our love of learning. They also keep us young when we share in any of their activities. As they continue to grow, we can share a wealth of knowledge to help expand their young minds. It is a pleasure to see them grow into young adults and work towards becoming productive citizens. And this all happens much faster than we wish.

PRAYER FOR THE BLESSING OF THE DAY...

Lord, today help me to see the world through the eyes of a child. Allow me to accept life with joy and enthusiasm. Even on my worst days, let me find a positive aspect of the day. Thank you for all the blessings You have given me. AMEN.

Stephanie Rehm

August 22

ONE LESSON I HAVE LEARNED IN MY LIFE IS...

A lesson I learned in life was the true meaning of trust by watching the reactions young children have when they see people they love. With outstretched arms and contagious laughter they run forward to greet them.

PRAYER FOR THE BLESSING OF THE DAY...

Lord, just today as You guide me through the day, free my mind of clutter and fill my heart with the joy and wonderment just like that of a young innocent child. As I focus my thoughts on You, allow me to see the world with a new awakening surrounded by all the beauty and design just as You planned. Let today be one of new discoveries for me as I view the world through the eyes of a trusting child. I pray that I may bring peace and happiness to at least one person and that I find a little bit of You in every place I go and in each individual I encounter today.

Anonymous

August 23

ONE LESSON I HAVE LEARNED IN MY LIFE IS...

Life is filled with storms. As I am writing this, we are in the middle of an Arizona monsoon storm. Dust, wind, and rain are all happening outside. And to make sure I am aware of it, the emergency warning just went off on my phone. The truth is, I enjoy a good monsoon this time of year.

Well, as far as I know, there are no storms in heaven. Heaven is beyond Camelot when it comes to perfection. Everything will be amazing -- no fears, no sorrows, no mistakes, no imperfections. It will be wonderful. But, in the meantime, I need to enjoy the monsoons, the rain, and the imperfections of life. They will only be with me for 80 years or so -- and then there will be plenty of perfection for us all.

PRAYER FOR THE BLESSING OF THE DAY...

Lord, help me to put up with traffic, rain, mistakes of others, and even my own mistakes. I want to enjoy this world, in all of its imperfections, to the fullest...and then come to the place of perfect peace with You. AMEN.

Fr. Dale

August 24

ONE LESSON I HAVE LEARNED IN MY LIFE IS...

The wedding feast at Cana is one of my favorite bible stories (John 2:1-11). It's not one of my favorites because I enjoy wine. It is one of my favorites because I want to enjoy life. And part of what I learn from this miracle is that our God is not a stuffy old codger who wants all of us to share in His misery. Rather, our God is vibrant and alive and He wants us to enjoy life and enjoy the fruits of His creation.

So many religions have portrayed God in a false way. He's not mean. He's not angry. He's not even a He. God is so far above any human portrayal or emotion we try to give to Him. God is love. God is energy. God is light, and life. God is mercy. God is joy.

God wants us to be part of His new reign of love in Jesus. The water into wine teaches that no Christian should ever have an ordinary life. We are called to a life of "fine wine" and extraordinary love.

PRAYER FOR THE BLESSING OF THE DAY...

Lord Jesus, let me be truly ALIVE with Your Spirit. Let me live life to the fullest. Let me live...until it is my time to live eternally with You. AMEN.

Fr. Dale

August 25

ONE LESSON I HAVE LEARNED IN MY LIFE IS...

Reading is a good thing. The great writer C.S. Lewis said, "You can never get a cup of tea large enough or a book long enough to suit me."

Spiritual reading is especially important. Books allow us to receive new ideas at our own pace. We can mark up a book, re-read a paragraph, or put the book down and reflect or pray about a new insight. I've heard it said that most Christians still have a second or third grade view of God. We need input. Groucho Marx said, "Outside of a dog, a book is a man's best friend." It's time for us all to make a new friend and read a book about God.

PRAYER FOR THE BLESSING OF THE DAY...

Heavenly Father, give me a hunger to know You. Allow me to desire to learn about YOU and Your ways. Open my eyes and my heart to new insights about what an awesome God You are. AMEN.

Fr. Dale

When Life Gives You **PINEAPPLES** *-- Make an Upside-down Cake!*

August 26

ONE LESSON I HAVE LEARNED IN MY LIFE IS…

I am not as strong as I think I am. I am stealing that line from one of my favorite Rich Mullins' songs. In fact, in my darkest time of life I listened to that song over and over. I reminded me that I was vulnerable and even the relationships I cherished most could be destroyed by lies and untruths. Rich says:

"Well it took the hand of God almighty

To part the waters of the sea

But it only took one little lie to separate you and me

Oh, we are not as strong,

As We Think We Are."

I am still not as strong as I would like to be. I often can't discipline myself to eat right. I don't stick with my intentions to read a daily devotional. I get tired, lazy, and sometimes discouraged.

But, God is strong. And God will be our strength even when we feel weak. He will give us grace and fortitude if we ask.

PRAYER FOR THE BLESSING OF THE DAY…

God, I am asking You to be my strength this day. I know I need You. Please Jesus, be with me. AMEN.

Fr. Dale

August 27

ONE LESSON I HAVE LEARNED IN MY LIFE IS…

Religion is good, but it doesn't make you holy. Humorist Garrison Keillor said, "Anyone who thinks sitting in church can make you a Christian must also think that sitting in a garage can make you a car."

I think the point is clear. Religion is only a tool to live out faith. Every

144

different religion offers its own insight to how best be faithful to God. But the goal is never religion. The goal is always God. We must seek to know God, love God, and serve God. Any religion worth its weight makes that clear. In real estate, it's all about location. In religion, it must be all about God's love.

PRAYER FOR THE BLESSING OF THE DAY...

Jesus, help me today to seek You above all else. May my simple prayer today be "Jesus first." AMEN.

Fr. Dale

August 28

ONE LESSON I HAVE LEARNED IN MY LIFE IS...

"The voice of truth says, 'DO NOT BE AFRAID!' And the voice of truth says, 'THIS IS FOR MY GLORY.' Out of all the voices calling out to me, I will choose to listen and believe the voice of truth."

These words from the Casting Crowns' song "Voice of Truth" inspire me to stand firm when all I want to do is crumble like a stale cookie. I heard the song right after we received some devastating news that left me facing a huge giant named "fear." All the hope I had wrapped around my weary, aching soul was ripped from my grasp and thrown out the window. My fear was like a vacuum that sucked me dry. Emptiness filled the space where hope once thrived. Despair consumed me. I couldn't breathe. My knees buckled. I felt lost...hopeless...and afraid.

Then I heard this song, and remembered a scripture verse that said ,"The Lord will not fail you or forsake you; do not fear." In that moment, I believed it. The truth plucked me from my darkness and I hung on for dear life to that thread of hope. And I prayed for a miracle. I called everyone on my speed dial and asked them to pray for a miracle with me. And then something wonderful happened. People started showing up. Family, friends, and our pastor arrived -- and with them the assurance that I wasn't alone. We hugged. We cried. We prayed. And the giant "fear" faded.

The Lord was with us that night. He is always here with us, as His Word promises. He never leaves; in fact He leads us through those dark hours of the night and into the light. He has taught me that there is always hope, even in the midst of devastation and loss. We just have to listen and believe the voice of our God, whose love for us is unconditional, and whose truth is eternal.

PRAYER FOR THE BLESSING OF THE DAY...

Lord, I pray today as David did in Psalm 25, "In You, Lord my God, I put my trust. Show me Your ways Lord. Guide me in Your truth and teach me, for You are God my Savior, and my hope is in You all day long." AMEN.

"The LORD is the one who goes ahead of you; He will be with you. He will not fail you or forsake you. Do not fear or be dismayed." (Deuteronomy 31:8)

Cheryl Armstrong

August 29

ONE LESSON I HAVE LEARNED IN MY LIFE IS...

There is always a way and enough to fit one more around the table.

PRAYER FOR THE BLESSING OF THE DAY...

Lord, there are so many hungry hearts that cannot be filled until our brothers and sisters are not starving before us. Help us reach into our own plates and feed the ones who can no longer raise their hands to their own mouths. Show us the way to multiply what we have until those who have nothing can live. Let us be the face of love to the destitute, and a voice of hope to those who have surrendered all that is truly human.

Jody Serey

August 30

ONE LESSON I HAVE LEARNED IN MY LIFE IS...

Acceptance. Growing up in a very conservative home, to a conservative family that pastors a very conservative church, acceptance was a concept that I really struggled to understand. Though my family and church preached that acceptance was something they held in high regard, they never really showed it. I can't really ever recall a time where a visitor to our church was never judged by at least one member of the church, and if they happened to be a known "sinner" -- forget about it. So growing up in that culture, I grew to be a very non-accepting young man.

PRAYER FOR THE BLESSING OF THE DAY...

Help me, Lord, to be a more accepting and non-judgmental person. Help me to show Your love to others. AMEN.

Emanuel Torres-Alarcon

August 31

ONE LESSON I HAVE LEARNED IN MY LIFE IS...

Silence never seems to come when I want it. When I want peace and quiet, it's never available. When I feel lonely or fearful and want distractions, it seems to be the middle of the night and it is silent. But as Christian song writer Matt Redman says, "Silence is a great environment to see and hear God." Somehow, we need to find moments to really listen to God who speaks in the silence of our hearts.

It is so important for us to know what God wants for us and from us. Silence is not the only way He speaks. His Spirit speaks through others, community, and events in our lives. But, silence is an essential point of our relationship with God.

PRAYER FOR THE BLESSING OF THE DAY...

Father, grant me some silence today. No matter when or where the silence comes, let me hear Your voice and see Your face. AMEN.

Fr. Dale

September 1

ONE LESSON I HAVE LEARNED IN MY LIFE IS...

It takes a village of people who love you and prayers to Jesus to help raise a great person.

PRAYER FOR THE BLESSING OF THE DAY...

Lord thank You for each day of learning about YOU!

Jadyn Kieny Broderson

September 2

ONE LESSON I HAVE LEARNED IN MY LIFE IS...

The word "awesome" is way over-used. The other day I was at a restaurant and ordered chicken strips. The waiter's response was "awesome." Trust me -- they were not!

However, when the term is used to describe God, it is accurately used. The more we meet God, or learn about Him, the more in AWE we become. And although things in this life might be good, or inspiring, or terrific, we would be wise to reserve the term "awesome" for God. God's Love, Power, and Mercy are overwhelming to us as human beings. Our response to God should be worship of God, and we should join the angels, saints, and all Creation in offering praise to our Creator. God is truly the only one worth our awe.

PRAYER FOR THE BLESSING OF THE DAY...

("Awesome God" by Rich Mullins)

"Our God is an Awesome God
He reigns from heaven above
with wisdom, power, and love
Our God is an Awesome God."

Fr. Dale

September 3

ONE LESSON I HAVE LEARNED IN MY LIFE IS...

My favorite book in the world is called Dangerous Wonder, written by a friend of mine, Michael Yaconelli (now deceased). Yaconelli wrote, "I want a lifetime of holy moments. Every day I want to be in dangerous proximity to Jesus. I long for a life that explodes with meaning and is filled with adventure, wonder, risk, and danger. I long for a faith that is gloriously treacherous."

I think my life, and maybe yours, is way too boring. Our spiritual lives should make us filled with new ideas, new thoughts, and new ways of seeing life.

PRAYER FOR THE BLESSING OF THE DAY...

God, wake me up today. Give me a sense of wonder at the creation You have given us. Let me be overjoyed today, that Your presence has filled my life. Give me Lord, a dangerous wonder that leads to amazing worship of You. AMEN.

Fr. Dale

September 4

ONE LESSON I HAVE LEARNED IN MY LIFE IS...

My September is a month filled with love and hope for the future. But for others it marks the end of the summer, the start of school, and a definite return to "normality" after the craziness of the summer. However, I've learned that life isn't about waiting for the storm to pass, but it's learning how to dance in the rain. So I never take life for granted. I try to live it to the best of my ability, because you never know what is around the corner.

PRAYER FOR THE BLESSING OF THE DAY...

Today as I face this day, never let a moment of hate or greed or hesitation fill me, but let the glory of Your compassion, God, fill my heart. I know that with faith, love and trust I will overcome each challenge that I meet this day. I am thankful, Lord, that You have blessed me with a warm caring heart.

Love is patient, love is kind. It does not envy, it does not boast, it is not rude, it is not self-seeking, it is not easily angered, it keeps no record of wrongs. Love does not delight in evil but rejoices with the truth. It always protects, always trusts, always hopes and always perseveres.

(1 Corinthians 13:4-7)

Weldon Turner

September 5

ONE LESSON I HAVE LEARNED IN MY LIFE IS...

I am thankful for my spouse. On this date, Stephanie and I got married in 1969. I call her my miracle bride as we met as pen pals. She was in Baltimore, Maryland and I was in Vietnam. I wrote a letter to a magazine called Hot Rod Cartoons asking for pen pals. In the next three months I received over 3,000 letters from women all over the USA. One of those letters was from Stephanie. I decided to write to five women, and the only letter I got in return was from Stephanie (how lucky for me). Stephanie had decided to write three GIs, and I was the only person to write her back.

I had idea when I started writing to Stephanie that I would begin to love her over the next seven months of writing almost every day. She told me her first husband was killed in Vietnam and she was a widow with a 13 month old daughter. I knew by Christmas that I was going to ask her to marry me when I came home. I got home March 24th, 1969 and stayed home a week. I bought a $25 dollar ticket from Chicago to Baltimore and met her for the first time on April 2. I will never forget what she was wearing – a midi skirt that was a blue and white checked jumper. She had long flowing hair that just flipped up as it touched her shoulder. I got off the plane and walked right past her. I thought that she would have been taller. She called my name and I turned and reached out to shake her hand and she stated, "Don't I deserve a hug?"

The next day I went to the Pentagon to get my orders changed from the 18th Airborne Corps at Ft. Bragg, NC to the Flight Surgeon's office at Davidson Airfield at Ft. Belvoir, VA. A bottle of Johnny Walker Red helped to get the orders changed. I asked her to marry me the next day and she said yes. We set a date for September 5, 1969.

We have faced many challenges and heart breaks over the years, but we faced them together with God helping us and guiding us. I had to go to Vietnam to meet my future bride. Who would have thought that something like this would happen to the both of us? Certainly not us. But I have learned to never say never when it comes to God. He has someone for each of us, and He made our connection for us. I truly believe that God is a God of miracles.

PRAYER FOR THE BLESSING OF THE DAY…

Dear Lord, thank you for giving me Stephanie as my wife. I have been so blessed with the help-mate You chose for me. How can I ever doubt Your love and care for me when You take care of me so well? AMEN.

Kerry Pardue

September 6

ONE LESSON I HAVE LEARNED IN MY LIFE IS…

Good science and good medicine only enrich faith. They do not harm it. I've heard people say "I really don't believe in God; I only believe in science and what I can prove."

I believe the more we learn about our world, our bodies, and our universe, the more we come to understand there is a DIVINE Creator who made it all. I also believe it is God who helps doctors and researchers help heal people from diseases. The brilliant scientist, Albert Einstein, said, "Science without religion is lame; religion without science is blind."

The ability to learn, to know, and to discover is God's gift to humankind. What we do with it becomes our gift back to God.

PRAYER FOR THE BLESSING OF THE DAY…

Father, help our doctors, researchers, and scientists to cure cancer, Alzheimer's, MS and other forms of illnesses. Give us knowledge that helps each human to enjoy the fullness of life. AMEN.

Fr. Dale

September 7

ONE LESSON I HAVE LEARNED IN MY LIFE IS…

The one lesson that I learned in my life was to turn it over to God and to trust completely in Him. Around 2:00 A.M. on Labor Day in 2013, my wife, Karen, was on the computer in our home office, which was on the other side of our house from our master bedroom. I had gone to bed earlier and had sleep-walked from my side of our very high

California king bed to my wife's side. I sat at the foot of the bed only to roll forward and land on my face, which awakened me as I heard my neck snap. At first I was confused, but knew that I had to turn this whole thing over to the Lord before I tried to do anything.

My prayer was short, and I discussed with Him how I had been turning my life over to His care daily and followed His will to the best of my ability. I asked Him to take over now and guide me, and if He wanted me now, I was ready! If not, I asked Him to show me how I could have more time here with Karen, our children and grandchildren. At that moment, a very strong, warm feeling started at my toes and very slowly advanced throughout my body to the very top of my head. Without a doubt in my mind, this was the Holy Spirit telling me to carefully reach for the poster of the bed and to gradually pull myself up to a standing position while keeping my head and neck as still as possible. As I did this, the warmth that had enveloped me slowly left by reversing its way down and out.

I continued praying knowing that the Lord was with me and that He was guiding the plethora of surgeons, physicians, nurses, therapists, and aides who helped me make a full recovery from my broken neck (C2) without being paralyzed. To this day, I thank the Lord for all that He has done and continues to do in my life, and I will always praise Him and thank Him for His gracious and generous love!

PRAYER FOR THE BLESSING OF THE DAY...

Lord, thank You for Your love and help me to interpret, achieve, and implement Your will daily in my life.

(Hebrews 20)

"Now may the God of Peace...That great Shepherd of the sheep... make You complete in every good work to do His will... through Jesus Christ to whom glory forever and ever." AMEN.

Reynold J. Krueger

September 8

ONE LESSON I HAVE LEARNED IN MY LIFE IS...

Living in Arizona has taught me how to protect myself from the harmful elements of desert living. During the hot summer months, I hunt for a shady spot to park my car. I take a bottle of water everywhere I go. I apply sunscreen before I brave the outdoors. I keep an umbrella in my glove box. Protection from harm is essential to my survival. God knows that. He knows my every need, my weaknesses and my vulnerabilities. And, because I am His, He has given His protection and provision to help me survive, with the promise that I will be okay.

My "life" verse – Romans 8:28 – has saved me time and time again, when I thought I couldn't survive the moment. "And we know that God causes all things to work together for good to those who love God, to those who are called according to His purpose." To those who are called according to HIS purpose…that's you and me. We are called by Him…chosen to follow Him, to seek after His righteousness, to love Him and to trust Him. But, that's not all. Because we are His, we reap all the blessings of being His! His promises are given to us and for us. His protection, provision and peace are OUR inheritance!

I am His child and when I am weak, I can cry out to Him, "Abba, Father" and He is already there. When I am weary, He is my strength. When I am scared, He is my comfort. When the weight of the world is consuming me, I can run to Him for shelter and be safe from the elements or any enemy that threatens my security.

PRAYER FOR THE BLESSING OF THE DAY…

Thank you, my God for calling me according to Your purpose. Thank you for Your promises that I cling to, trusting that all will be well… even before I know the outcome. Thank you for revealing in Your Word, who YOU ARE and how You provide for my every need. Help me to seek You in all things and trust in Your protection.

"From the end of the earth I will cry to You, when my heart is overwhelmed; Lead me to the rock that is higher than I, for You have been a shelter for me, a strong tower from the enemy." (Psalm 61:2-3)

"The name of the LORD is a strong tower; the righteous run to it and are safe." (Proverbs 18:10)

Cheryl Armstrong

September 9

ONE LESSON I HAVE LEARNED IN MY LIFE IS...

I realized that Jesus gave up His life for me. Oh I've heard this many, many times throughout my 71 years, but today it hit me between the eyes. I was reading Max Lucado's book GRACE. In it, a prison guard is talking to Barabbas: "You're free to go. They took Jesus instead of you."

Wow. What an impact. Jesus took on insurmountable suffering for me. What love! Think about it -- You're free to go. They took Jesus instead of you.

PRAYER FOR THE BLESSING OF THE DAY...

Thank you, Jesus, for loving me so much.

"For God loved the world so much that He gave His only son." (John 3:16)

Camille Heniger

September 10

ONE LESSON I HAVE LEARNED IN MY LIFE IS...

Someday there will be a morning when the sun comes up without me. There will be a night when the moonlight does not reach my window.

PRAYER FOR THE BLESSING OF THE DAY...

Lord, let me live each moment in gratitude. Help me measure out my days with thankfulness that I was able to wrap the hours around me. Help me celebrate every good moment I encounter, without needing to measure like salt the amount of joy You have given me to be certain that I have been given my fair share.

Jody Serey

September 11

ONE LESSON I HAVE LEARNED IN MY LIFE IS...

What I have learned is one event can change history forever. I remember standing and watching the early morning news as we found out

154

that a plane crashed into the World Trade Center in New York. Later the world would find out that this was no ordinary plane crash, but a selfish act of terrorism that changed our nation and our world forever. Throughout this day in 2001, lives were lost and people were left wondering and searching for answers. Ironically, people were being drawn into churches, standing united as a nation, seeking out God and His compassion and love...

Jesus' event over 2000 years earlier helps all of us understand the day that changed our lives. It was one that is not focused on an act of terror, but instead one that is focused on love.

Jesus laid down his life so that you and I can live. He sacrificed everything so that we could be healed and be reconciled by His love. We will have many events that are mileposts in our lives. Our weddings our birthdays, our graduations, or the birth of our children. Major events that always point us back to the love of God.

When we are searching for answers in our lives, may we end the confusion by coming to the Lord and the only real truth that makes sense -- His unconditional love.

PRAYER FOR THE BLESSING OF THE DAY...

Father, please let me seek out Your love and guidance through difficult times in my life. When I cannot understand the ways of the world, let me turn to You for Your mercy and love.

"Come to me all who are weary and find life burdensome, and I will refresh You says the Lord. Take my yoke upon Your shoulders and learn from me for I am gentle and yoke is easy and burden light." (Matthew 11)

Mark Dippre

September 12

ONE LESSON I HAVE LEARNED IN MY LIFE IS...

That no matter what, life does go on. Yesterday was the anniversary of the planes crashing into the World Trade Center. At the time (9-11), it seemed very dark and like the whole world had changed. No doubt, the world did change that day. But, it didn't end. Life does go on. We can live through tragedy, war, illness, and even the deaths of loved ones. The human spirit is strong and resilient. And with God's grace, we do rise again. I remember reading a description of the resurrection which simply said "Dear God, You mean I survived that!"

Never underestimate the power of God mixed with the human will. It is a power that is far stronger than anything evil can ever throw at us.

PRAYER FOR THE BLESSING OF THE DAY...

Thank you, God for a new day.

Thank you for a new opportunity to live and to love.

Thank you for never allowing us to give in.

Fr. Dale

September 13

ONE LESSON I HAVE LEARNED IN MY LIFE IS...

I have two questions for God. My first one, is "Are You pleased with me for what I do for You?"

I try to be loving husband, father and friend to those I associate with. I try to be a try to treat all with love and respect. I share my resources with family and friends and with You, God. I give of time, talent and support as my gift to You.

The second question is, "Are You pleased with who I am?"

I try hard to give to You my best, but included are times I get angry, show interest in myself before others. I am human like everyone else, and guilty of putting worldly things ahead of You at times.

PRAYER FOR THE BLESSING OF THE DAY...

Lord, I know You love me regardless of what I do and who I am. I see You in all that is good in my life and I know You are standing by when I falter. You are waiting as I grow in faith. For we are Your workman-ship, created in Christ Jesus to do good works, which You prepare in advance for us to do. (from Ephesians 2:10)

Robert Dube

September 14

ONE LESSON I HAVE LEARNED IN MY LIFE IS...

I have learned the importance of the cross. I have over 50 crosses hanging in my small condo. It is a great collection and everywhere I look I am reminded of the importance Christ has in my life.

In many churches, today is the Feast of the Triumph of the Cross. It is a day to celebrate that the Cross is not a sign of death or defeat, but a sign of victory. In His cross, we have all been saved.

This date was chosen because the original Church of the Holy Sepulcher was dedicated in 335. What they believed to be the true cross was brought out for all the people to venerate.

PRAYER FOR THE BLESSING OF THE DAY...

Jesus, each time I see a cross, may I be grateful for Your incredible love. May I come to understand and accept the gift of Your unconditional love for me. Amen

Fr. Dale

September 15

ONE LESSON I HAVE LEARNED IN MY LIFE IS...

God is truly in control. Many times I have been frustrated by events that have not fallen into place in my time or way. Sometimes they are big events, and at other times they are small. Looking back when things have not gone my way, I usually find out that there was some kind of reason for the better that my way was not in God's time.

I also know that God helps those who help themselves. When struggling with something, I know that I need to pray to God and ask for assistance. He usually helps me, but I have to work through the issue or problem also.

I have been blessed to have worked for seven years in Vacation Bible School and have a collection of that music. The first thing I do each day is spend a half hour using that music as my prayer. I also spend the last half hour of my evening listening to the music and giving thanks for the day, including all of its blessings and challenges.

PRAYER FOR THE BLESSING OF THE DAY...

Lord, help me to remember that I am not God. You know what my life holds and You alone unfold that mystery to me on a daily basis. Help me do whatever You ask. Forgive me if I have wronged You or others in any way. AMEN.

Stephanie Rehm

September 16

ONE LESSON I HAVE LEARNED IN MY LIFE IS...

Anxiety is not a pleasant experience. I went through a period of my life when I actually had anxiety attacks. They physically felt like a heart attack. Emotionally they made me full of fear and negativity. I don't think God desired for me to feel any of these things.

Anxiety is a feeling of worry, nervousness, or unease. Sometimes it has to do with an upcoming event and sometimes it comes from simply feeling overwhelmed with life. As Christians, we must turn our fears and concerns over to Jesus. He can handle them. And, we can trust Him. Worry and anxiety never help a situation. Faith and trust in God always helps tremendously.

PRAYER FOR THE BLESSING OF THE DAY...

(Philippians 4:6-7)

"Do not be anxious about anything, but in everything, by prayer and petition, with thanksgiving, present our requests to God. And the peace of God, which is beyond all understanding, will guard your hearts and your minds in Christ Jesus."

Fr. Dale

September 17

ONE LESSON I HAVE LEARNED IN MY LIFE IS...

That anger doesn't really work. I understand what it is -- and how it is a secondary emotion. When something or someone seems out of control, anger gives a feeling of power and control. But in the long run all it does is destroy you and the people surrounding you. The word anger comes from the root word angst. It literally means to "choke." When you get angry, you tend to choke everything. I know that Jesus got angry in the temple. I know there is a place for anger. I also know I am not as wise as Jesus in being able to choose the right times.

PRAYER FOR THE BLESSING OF THE DAY...

Father, help me let go of any anger I feel towards myself, others, and the world. Help me to choose to love even when I feel hurt or out of control. AMEN.

Fr. Dale

September 18

ONE LESSON I HAVE LEARNED IN MY LIFE IS...

First off, everybody lives life without a "how to" book revealing how to get through day-to-day trials. No one is born knowing how to walk or talk; we have to learn over time. I didn't grow up in the greatest environment, but through my circumstances I've learned that patience is a virtue worth waiting for. The longer you wait for patience to find you, the more you will gain. I've also learned to stand up for myself and that you can't let people bring you down. Life is too short to let anger and disappointment rule you. Nobody said life was easy; in fact, it's harder than you think. But in the end, you might find that going through hard times makes those good moments exceptional.

PRAYER FOR THE BLESSING OF THE DAY...

Dear Jesus,

Please lift up Your compassion to cover me and my heart! Be with me and show me Your plans for my life. Remind me of Your promise to take care of me, and give me strength when I'm afraid. In Your name I pray. AMEN.

Richard Lodge

September 19

ONE LESSON I HAVE LEARNED IN MY LIFE IS...

Miracles did not just happen in the bible. Miracles happen every day if we open our eyes to see them. The New Testament is filled with the miracles Jesus performed. Through Jesus the sick were healed, the blind were cured, and the hungry were fed. But His greatest miracle was on the cross when He forgave us all of our sins.

The miracles that happen today are not too different from them. Today, someone forgives for a hurt that happened years ago. Today, for the first time, someone gave to a food bank. Today, through prayer and medicine, someone was healed. Just look around – miracles are happening.

PRAYER FOR THE BLESSING OF THE DAY...

(Luke 7:20-23)

"Are you the one who is to come or are we to wait for another? Jesus had just cured many people of diseases, plagues, evil spirits, and had given sight to many who were blind. So he replied to the messengers, 'Go back and report to John what you have seen and heard: The blind receive sight, the lame walk, those who have leprosy are cleansed, the deaf hear, the dead are raised, and the good news is proclaimed to the poor. Blessed is anyone who does not stumble on account of me.'"

Fr. Dale

September 20

ONE LESSON I HAVE LEARNED IN MY LIFE IS...

I really don't like "drama.". I know most movies and TV shows are based on some type of drama, and it is fine for entertainment purposes. But in real life, "drama" tends to be destructive. It seems like we all have a "drama" queen or king in our lives. As I age, I am getting much less tolerant of them.

What do I mean by "drama"? The events of life can be dramatic in themselves. But, some folks take a paper cut and turn it into a shark bite. They take every event, personalize it, and then blow it out of pro-

160

portion. Then all of the attention is on them and no longer on the event. I say ENOUGH of that! It is time to put things back into perspective.

PRAYER FOR THE BLESSING OF THE DAY...

Lord, help me to be a good, honest, real person of faith. Help me to always look for the blessings in the events of life. AMEN.

Fr. Dale

September 21

ONE LESSON I HAVE LEARNED IN MY LIFE IS...

There is no substitute for being there in person.

PRAYER FOR THE BLESSING OF THE DAY...

Lord, the next time I say, "If there's anything I can do, just let me know," please knock me off my horse. Don't let me walk away from the broken so I can avoid meeting their gaze or hearing their sighs. Make me think of ways to be useful, to be kind, to be of comfort. Do not let me retreat from what makes me uncomfortable, or tries my patience. Drag my hands out of my lap and put them to work.

Jody Serey

September 22

ONE LESSON I HAVE LEARNED IN MY LIFE IS...

Attitude matters. I choose a lot of what I feel, experience, and react to. Christian evangelist Charles Swindoll said, "The longer I live, the more I realize the impact of attitude on life. Attitude is more important than facts."

Swindoll is right. I can choose to see the negative or hear the negative instead of the positive. I can choose to whine about my bad fortune. I can choose to blame others instead of holding myself accountable. I have the power to choose my attitude and my thoughts.

Pastor Swindoll also said, "I am convinced that life is 10% what happens to me and 90% how I react to it."

If that is true, and I believe it is, than 9/10 of my happiness today will depend on me and my reactions. So…when I tell myself to "have a nice day," I really do have control to make it happen.

PRAYER FOR THE BLESSING OF THE DAY…

Father, let me make good choices today, especially by choosing to have a good attitude.

AMEN.

Fr. Dale

September 23

ONE LESSON I HAVE LEARNED IN MY LIFE IS…

Every choice we make adds to our strengths and our weaknesses. Our job here on earth is to build our room in heaven. We need to live a life that is leading to an eternal life.

PRAYER FOR THE BLESSING OF THE DAY…

Lord, please send us wisdom. We want to walk in your path daily and lead others to do the same. This is the gift we desire the most.

Pat and Sue Kieny

September 24

ONE LESSON I HAVE LEARNED IN MY LIFE IS…

We are supposed to "dismiss all anxiety from our minds" -- at least that is what St. Paul said in his letter to the Philippians. Great suggestion! I just know for me, it's not easy to do. We should do two things: (1) rejoice, and (2) present our needs to God.

If I work at it, I can do those things. I can rejoice when I choose to focus on the blessings of life instead of the trials. And, I can offer my needs to God knowing that He is my parent who always loves me and cares for me.

I have had an anxiety attack a few times in my life. It feels like a heart attack. Your heart begins to race, the fear begins to overcome and it is hard to breathe. But there is a better option -- and that is GOD.

PRAYER FOR THE BLESSING OF THE DAY...

(Philippians 4:4-7)

Rejoice in the Lord always! I will say it again. Rejoice!

Everyone should see how unselfish you are. The Lord himself is near. Dismiss all anxiety from your minds. Present your needs to God in every form of prayer and in petitions full of gratitude. Then God's own peace, which is beyond all understanding, will stand guard over your hearts and minds, in Christ Jesus. AMEN.

Fr. Dale

September 25

ONE LESSON I HAVE LEARNED IN MY LIFE IS...

Loving is a decision. We all have people in our lives, especially family, who we clearly LOVE. The problem is that sometimes we really don't like those people. Sometimes our loved ones become self-centered. Sometimes our loved ones become bitter or angry. And sometimes our loved ones struggle with addictions. But our job as Christians is to still offer unconditional LOVE. There is no place in the bible that mentions unconditional like.

PRAYER FOR THE BLESSING OF THE DAY...

Father, You are the God of unconditional love. I ask You to help me become an instrument of that love. Help me to see others with Your eyes so that I can love them with Your heart. AMEN.

Fr. Dale

September 26

ONE LESSON I HAVE LEARNED IN MY LIFE IS...

Unconditional love is not the same thing as unconditional agreement. When we say God loves us no matter what, we are feeling the truth.

But that doesn't mean God agrees or approves of our bad behavior. God is big enough to see beyond our bad decisions.

We must do the same for each other. I don't need to approve, affirm, or even accept the decisions of someone I love. Violence, hatred, and immorality are not acceptable to me. But, the person is still LOVABLE.

Spiritual writer Henri Nouwen says, "God's unconditional love means that God continues to love us even when we say or think evil things."

God is patient. He waits for us to return to Him and to His great love. When we say God is love, we mean everything about God is love.

PRAYER FOR THE BLESSING OF THE DAY...

Lord, knowing I am beloved should change everything about me... including my behavior, my choices, and my commitment to be true to You. AMEN.

Fr. Dale

September 27

ONE LESSON I HAVE LEARNED IN MY LIFE IS...

Robert Frost said in "Death of the Hired Man", "Home is the place where, when you have to go there, they have to take you in...I should have called it something you somehow haven't to deserve."

So is anything we dare to call "church."

PRAYER FOR THE BLESSING OF THE DAY...

Lord, help me find You in the buildings that claim to be Your places of worship. Let me also make those welcome who come in search of You any place that I might be. Steer me away from passing judgment or finding fault with anyone who seeks You. And what I cannot understand, help me to accept as one of Your pilgrims.

Jody Serey

September 28

ONE LESSON I HAVE LEARNED IN MY LIFE IS...

The lessons are many, ongoing, and endless. Learning is a verb and not a noun. A movement ever dynamic and usually challenging.

Lately, I have come to experience our God as the Divine Dance Instructor and to see myself as the sometimes willing, often reluctant, and always stumbling apprentice.

I have come to understand the profound reality that lives and moves and has being as a mysterious and alluring Cosmic Dance. The term is borrowed from the great 20th century mystic Thomas Merton who says, "Indeed, we are in the midst of it [the dance], and it is in the midst of us, for it beats in our very blood, whether we want it or not." This metaphor has taken root in my own life.

I have done my fair share of standing in the audience watching others dancing jigs, cha-chas, tangos, and waltzes. Today, I feel a palpable invitation to step into the dance. The steps, music, and rhythm are amazingly familiar. There is a knowing, but I have simply neglected practicing. If only I begin to move my feet...the choreography will come in time. Soon, I suspect, I will be the dance.

PRAYER FOR THE BLESSING OF THE DAY...

Grand Dancer and Mover of All Being, open my ears to Your Heavenly Harmony, keep me to cast my eyes not on my feet, but on Your lead. May I trust Your Sacred Instructions, answer Your Holy Invitation and place myself in Your Wise Apprenticeship. Remove all fear of stumbling, rather filling my dance book with Your grace. Use my clumsiness as an example that others may be drawn into the Great Dance.

"Let them praise His Name with dancing and make music to Him with tambourines and harps." (Psalm 149:3)

"For in Him we live and move and have our being" (Acts 17:28)

Karen C. Klemens

September 29

ONE LESSON I HAVE LEARNED IN MY LIFE IS...

Freeway traffic is annoying. I was recently stuck in a long back-up as I was driving to church. The whole time I was standing still, all I could think of was being late and getting behind. When I finally got to the scene of the accident, I could see a car completely over-turned and someone had died. I thought I was having a BAD day! Another family was hurting much worse than I was.

PRAYER FOR THE BLESSING OF THE DAY...

Lord, help me keep my life in perspective. There are so many others who are hungry, hurt, dying, lost, and alone. Be with all who need You, Lord. And instead of focusing on myself, allow me to be joined in prayer with those who need You most.

Fr. Dale

September 30

ONE LESSON I HAVE LEARNED IN MY LIFE IS...

Life is what you make of it. Look around. The people who claim to have miserable lives are always acting miserable. You would never hear a happy person say their life is worthless. They might go through hard times, but they tend to look on the bright side of things. There is always a point in our lives where we have to choose how we view things, so why not choose to think positive?

PRAYER FOR THE BLESSING OF THE DAY...

Dear Jesus, help me to remember to have a positive outlook on life, no matter what situation I'm in.

Cassidy Palmer

October 1

ONE LESSON I HAVE LEARNED IN MY LIFE IS...

It is important to be creative. Children use their imaginations to create. Young adults use their energy and talents to come up with new ideas.

But, once many of us hit middle age (and older), we begin to think our creative days are over. I do not that is the way God meant it to work. As we age and add experience and wisdom into our lives, it is important to never stop creating. At any age, we can think new thoughts, embrace new styles, and come up with new solutions. I guess that is why the expression "young at heart" was created.

PRAYER FOR THE BLESSING OF THE DAY...

Father, as I see Your creation today -- the sun, moon, stars, mountains, trees, and people -- may I be reminded that I was made in Your image and likeness. So, Lord, let me think with a new freshness and allow me to create anything to Your glory.

Fr. Dale

October 2

ONE LESSON I HAVE LEARNED IN MY LIFE IS...

That we need to learn to forgive and let go.

As a parent raising four children, I am amazed at the vast amount of emotions that play out throughout the day. One minute they are all getting along great and then, the very next, there is all out war. Children go through emotions quickly, but they also reconcile quickly. A quick hug, or the words of "I'm sorry" can turn all those emotions of anger back into love.

I think that grown-ups should take a lesson from their children. We all too often hold onto hurt feelings, anger and painful events in our lives. Sometimes those walls that we build up in our relationships become so high, we forget how they started in the first place.

Jesus reminds us in the scriptures, "Let the children come to me..." and reminds all of us to become childlike again. His message is that of mercy and forgiveness. Today, let us say those simple words, and let go of some hurt and renew a friendship. It could be the best thing we have ever done.

(Mark 10:13-16)

PRAYER FOR THE BLESSING OF THE DAY...

Father, let me have the heart of a child and share the mercy and love
You desire. May I use the gift of Your mercy and love to renew the
world with Your love. AMEN.

Mark Dippre

October 3

ONE LESSON I HAVE LEARNED IN MY LIFE IS...

According to Andrew Murray, author of Humility, we need to allow the
Holy Spirit to convict us of our prideful ways. The correct attitude we
need to have before God is humility, surrendering our lives to God's
will and placing our entire dependence on Him. Humility is acknowledging the truth of our positions as sons and daughters of God and
yielding to His Almighty authority and power. Humility comes only
through God's grace to us. It is not easily attained and must be sought
through consistent prayer, faith and practice. Imagine it to be a lifelong
effort!

PRAYER FOR THE BLESSING OF THE DAY...

Lord, make me aware of all the ways I am prideful in my thoughts,
words, and actions. Guard me against my inflated ego, help me to be
humble, not just to try to appear humble. Whatever good I am able
to do is because You empower me. I do nothing on my own. This I
KNOW, and for this knowledge I ought to glorify You far better than I
do. By Your grace, make me fully know the truth of the humility that
can change my character and make me more like Your blessed Son,
Jesus.

Suzanne Cline

October 4

ONE LESSON I HAVE LEARNED IN MY LIFE IS...

Once we bring a life into this world, we must PROTECT it.
For a child is a body, and an eternal soul that belongs to God.
God lends us our children...and one day will bring us and all his chil-
dren home to Heaven.

When Life Gives You **PINEAPPLES** *-- Make an Upside-down Cake!*

PRAYER FOR THE BLESSING OF THE DAY...

May we seek to know Your will, Lord, and do it. May we be kind and helpful to everyone always, especially those who challenge us. Give us grace to smile, be patient, remain calm, and carry on in love.

May the Holy Spirit help us to forgive, be thankful in all circumstances, and let God be in charge of our and others' lives. Keep us aware of Your great love for us, Lord, and open our hearts to grow in love for You and others.

Jerry and Sue Cline

October 5

ONE LESSON I HAVE LEARNED IN MY LIFE IS...

It's not that hard to make someone else feel good. Little girls smile when you call them "beautiful." Young boys beam when you refer to them as a "superman." But adults respond the best when you say "good job" or compliment them in some way. As a matter of fact, a written thank you note, a little extra tip, or a sincere "God bless you" can make someone's day.

The fact is, honoring someone else costs us very little. And it can turn someone's negative day into a much better one.

Why should we make someone else's day? Because God does it for us all the time. A sunset, a falling star, a cool breeze can be a sign of God's love. God affirms us...and we pay it forward. The more we look for signs of God's love...the more we can consciously pass it on.

PRAYER FOR THE BLESSING OF THE DAY...

Open my eyes, Lord, to see Your many signs of love. Help me to pass Your love and affirmation on to others. AMEN.

Fr. Dale

October 6

ONE LESSON I HAVE LEARNED IN MY LIFE IS...

We are all hypocrites. I had a college professor who told us that she was going to write a book called In Defense of Hypocrisy. She went

on to say that every parent, coach, teacher, and pastor teaches people
to do things better than they ever did them. They each teach people
not to make the mistakes they have made and encourage others to be
better and accomplish more than they have been able to accomplish.
My professor's insights were accurate. However, there is a lot more to
say about hypocrisy. Jesus himself condemned it in the Pharisees when
they laid burdens on other people they were unwilling to accept for
themselves. And, I believe, he condemns it in us when we judge other
people and at the same time, fail to live up to the standards we hold for
others. We cannot be doing, saying, and thinking things that are contrary to Christ at the same time we are pledging out allegiance to Him.
We must stop judging others, take a good honest look at ourselves,
and with God's grace, begin to change the things in our lives that are
contrary to the Gospel.

PRAYER FOR THE BLESSING OF THE DAY...

(Matthew 6: 5-6)

"And when you pray, do not be like the hypocrites, for they love to
pray standing in the synagogues and on the street corners to be seen
by others. Truly I tell you, they have received their reward in full. But
when you pray, go into your room, close the door and pray to your Father, who is unseen. Then your Father, who sees what is done in secret,
will reward you."

Fr. Dale

October 7
ONE LESSON I HAVE LEARNED IN MY LIFE IS...

Happy endings are rare. Most endings are accompanied by a certain
amount of sadness – especially if there hasn't been a chance to say
goodbye.

PRAYER FOR THE BLESSING OF THE DAY...

Lord, help me accept the natural ebbs and flows of daily living. Help
me understand that many things are not mine to fix, and some things
are inevitable --no matter how hard I fight, or how deeply I deny.

Jody Serey

October 8

ONE LESSON I HAVE LEARNED IN MY LIFE IS...

One of my favorite quotes is, "We have the freedom of the children of God."

But, are we really free? Sometimes it feels like we are trapped in our bad choices and struggles. Sometimes too, stress, depression, and darkness can feel overwhelming.

Scripture is right. We are free! No matter what the world says to us, we have God's freedom. People can take away our exterior freedom. No one can take away our interior freedom.

Over the years different denominations have limited freedom. Some denominations say we aren't free to drink or dance. Catholics often don't feel free to think on their own. Some fundamentalists act like we aren't free to be happy. None of this comes from God; it comes from some religious leaders.

The Holy Spirit frees us to laugh, to give, to have joy, to learn, to seek, and ultimately to love. We are free to be creative, experiment with art and music, and to have passion. We are free to praise and worship God. Because we are the children of God – we are free!

PRAYER FOR THE BLESSING OF THE DAY...

Lord, always let me celebrate my freedom by following Christ and by choosing to love. AMEN.

Fr. Dale

October 9

ONE LESSON I HAVE LEARNED IN MY LIFE IS...

Have you ever found yourself in a situation where you have a number of choices and you just can't figure out what to choose, or where to go from where you are? I've found myself in that spot numerous times during my life, where I just can't decide what step to take next. During those times I tended to feel lonely, anxious, frustrated, and sometimes even apathetic.

The Christian answer in those times is always the same: pray. Pray for God to direct our steps. Pray for God to give us clarity. Pray for God to tell us what to do. And while that is all well and good, what I've come to find is sometimes God just wants us to choose. God has given you the ability to choose. He's given friends and family to advise us, intellect and resources to make an informed decision, and He's given the Bible as an example and tool to help us navigate life successfully. He's given us everything we need, so why are we still uneasy?

The answer is simple: we're scared. We are terrified that if we make the wrong decision, something terrible will happen. Or worse, that we'd miss out on a great opportunity. The problem with this way of thinking is that we end up using God as a crutch. We ask, "God, tell me where I should go to school? Who should I marry? Should I accept this new job that would make me move?"

What happens if we wait too long and the opportunity disappears? We might say, "I guess that it wasn't God's will."

But what if we jump on the opportunity and aren't happy with the outcome? We may end up getting mad at God. "God why have You brought me here? Why have You abandoned me?"

This is not fair to God. We serve God who loves us. A God who showers us in mercy and who loves to pour out His blessings on us. It is unfair for us to blame Him just because we aren't happy with how things turned out.

In the past, I've jumped on opportunities that I thought were great, but after awhile I realized that it wasn't where I wanted to be. That doesn't mean that God didn't use the time for good. If we start doubting our choices and wondering "what if", we won't be able to see the new blessings God has sent our way. Doubt will always come. When it does, we just need to remember that God is with us, and will always be with us. He can and will use any situation for His glory. So when you don't know what to choose or what step to take next, you can rest assured that no matter what you choose, God will be there with you.

PRAYER FOR THE BLESSING OF THE DAY...

God, help me to use what You have given me to help guide me through the tough choices in life. Help me to trust that You will be with me, and that You will be glorified in whatever happens. Help me to have peace about my choices and help me to learn from my mistakes. God, my life is Yours, and I want to be the best that I can be for You. In Your name I pray. AMEN.

David Person

October 10

ONE LESSON I HAVE LEARNED IN MY LIFE IS...

God is a lot bigger, more powerful, and more awesome that I used to think.

Years ago I read a book called Your God is Too Small, by J.B. Phillips. Phillips, who died in 1983, was an Anglican canon. The premise of his book is that most of us have a view of God which limits who He is and hence limits how we believe God interacts in our lives. Over the years, I have sat across the desk from many folks and have said to them, "Your view of God is way too small." Little did I know that I, too, had a small view of an immense God.

One of my favorite quotes from Phillips' book is, "No denomination has a monopoly on God's grace, and none has an exclusive recipe for producing Christian character. It is quite plain to even the disinterested observer that the real God takes no notice whatsoever of the boxes we put Him in, and is subject to no regulation of man."

In my narrow view of God, I believed that God visited lots of places, but that He dwelled in the church as I knew it.

I have come to realize that NO ONE speaks for God. And yet, WE ALL speak for God. No one person, no one office, no one member of the clergy always speaks for God. Sometimes they speak only for themselves. And sometimes great sinners and small children unknowingly speak for the Almighty. We cannot contain or control who God is and how God chooses to reveal Himself.

PRAYER FOR THE BLESSING OF THE DAY...

(Ephesians 6:10)

"Be strong in the Lord and in the strength of His might." Open my heart to hear You, see You, and love You. AMEN.

Fr. Dale

October 11

ONE LESSON I HAVE LEARNED IN MY LIFE IS...

Even if your parents have been gone for many years, you still miss them with the heart of an orphan.

PRAYER FOR THE BLESSING OF THE DAY...

Lord, in an era shaped by the blaming of all of life's misfortunes on one's childhood and parents, let me remember my family with gratitude. Help me remember that every parent begins as an amateur mother or father, and mistakes are bound to be made. I ask that my own children look back at with me with kindness and compassion, and forgive me for the times I failed them because the best I could do fell short of what was needed. Father of all of us, I ask for wisdom and mercy.

Jody Serey

October 12

ONE LESSON I HAVE LEARNED IN MY LIFE IS...

I am my own worst enemy. I sometimes allow my thoughts and self-talk to take me deep into self-pity, self-doubt, and depression. My only hope is to cry out to God.

[Psalm 42:6-8 The Message (MSG)]

When my soul is in the dumps, I rehearse
    everything I know of You.
From Jordan depths to Hermon heights,
    including Mount Mizar.
Chaos calls to chaos,
    to the tune of whitewater rapids.
Your breaking surf, Your thundering breakers
    Crash and crush me.
Then God promises to love me all day,
    sing songs all through the night!

    My life is God's prayer.

PRAYER FOR THE BLESSING OF THE DAY...

Lord, hear my cries of desperation. You are my only hope, rescue, and salvation. Lord save me from myself and self-destruction. You have made me in Your image. Teach me, fill me with Your presence, help me grow into Your likeness. AMEN.

Carol Taylor

October 13

ONE LESSON I HAVE LEARNED IN MY LIFE IS...

Kids only get one childhood. If there is anything, big or small, any of us could do to make a better life for a child, we should do it. The great thing about most kids is they are pretty simple. An act of kindness can go a long way for a child. It seems to me that when I was a kid, although life wasn't perfect, it was good. We had fun. Children today have way too many pressures. They lose their innocence too early. If any of us can bring joy to a child today, it will be well received by them -- and by God.

PRAYER FOR THE BLESSING OF THE DAY...

(Matthew 19: 13-15)

"Then people brought little children to Jesus for him to place his hands on them and pray for them. But the disciples rebuked them. Jesus said, 'Let the little children come to me, and do not hinder them, for the kingdom of heaven belongs to such as these.' When he had placed his hands on them, he went on from there."

Fr. Dale

October 14

ONE LESSON I HAVE LEARNED IN MY LIFE IS...

One of the most powerful lessons I have adopted in my life is that "when you change the way you look at things, the things you look at change." This has helped me see God's hand in everything I do and in all that happens on my earthly journey. Where I used to see coincidence or luck, I now find Divine order, life's lessons and guidance.

PRAYER FOR THE BLESSING OF THE DAY...

Lord, I thank You for revealing Your Divine plan in everything I do and in all that happens in my life. Instead of finding fault, I now experience joy in knowing that I am loved continually by You and protected and guided by Your Holy Spirit.

Greg Fyten

October 15

ONE LESSON I HAVE LEARNED IN MY LIFE IS...

I should follow the "promptings" I feel, more often. We all get those inner nudges from time to time. I believe a lot of those come from the Holy Spirit. Sometimes I feel prompted to call someone to see how they are doing. Whenever I follow the nudge, it seems to be for the better. The other day I was in a restaurant having breakfast with a friend. At the next table was a young Marine with who appeared to be his mother. I wanted to pay their bill and thank him for serving. My nephew is a Marine and he makes me very proud. However, I didn't because the person I was with would have thought I was silly. My mistake! I should have done what God prompted me to do.

PRAYER FOR THE BLESSING OF THE DAY...

Lord, send me Your Holy Spirit. Prompt me to do acts of love and service throughout the day. And then Lord, give me the courage to follow through. AMEN.

Fr. Dale

October 16

ONE LESSON I HAVE LEARNED IN MY LIFE IS...

The "Good Old Days' weren't really that great. After knowing a world filled with polio, and then living in one without it and myriad other diseases and risks, there is no way I would want to go back in time. (But I will listen to any and all Beatles music.)

176

PRAYER FOR THE BLESSING OF THE DAY...

Lord, help me appreciate what I don't have to do today. I don't have to walk miles for water, I don't have to watch helpless as my family starves, I don't have to survive another day in chains in a foreign prison. Let me realize at every turn that I am blessed beyond all measure even before my feet touch the floor, and I am no more worthy than any other of the ones on this planet. Fill me with gratitude, and then put me to work.

Jody Serey

October 17

ONE LESSON I HAVE LEARNED IN MY LIFE IS...

"Heavenly Father" was always hard for me to say.

Never having experienced a father in my life, it was hard for me to relate to a Heavenly Father.

It was a long time before I realized that I was hung up on the name "father," and that I was missing out on the many blessings and the unconditional love God had for me.

Although our relationship with our earthly fathers may be disappointing or even nonexistent, it's comforting to know that our Heavenly Father is always with us and He never fails.

PRAYER FOR THE BLESSING OF THE DAY...

(1 John 3:1)

"See what great love the Father has lavished upon us, that we may be called children of God! AMEN.

David Reiter

October 18

ONE LESSON I HAVE LEARNED IN MY LIFE IS...

Three simple one-syllable words mean so much when they come from the heart...

When is the last time you said "I love you" to someone? Maybe to your husband or wife this morning or before you went off to work. Maybe it was to a child or grandchild who just needed a little extra boost. This simple phrase is powerful when it comes from the heart. In fact, they are kisses from Heaven.

Christians believe that God is the source of all love. Did you ever stop to think that if we are seeing something that moves us so much that we want to say the words "I love you" to them, we are indeed encountering a GOD MOMENT. My grandfather use to call such experiences a "kiss from Heaven." I learned from him to make sure that I say them often so that message of HIS LOVE is never forgotten.

I love to see what those words do when they are being said. My wife stops and smiles because she knows that we are in it together. My children feel a connection and a shield of protection as they go forth to the daily activities planned for the day. A co-worker or friends find the real value that they hold in my life.

Three simple words are so powerful. Jesus reminds us that we are called to send forth his message of LOVE. The greatest way that I think we can do that is by not being stingy in saying those words, but by living them and telling those close to our heart, "I LOVE YOU."

(John 15:13)

"No greater love than this then to lay down a life for a friend."

PRAYER FOR THE BLESSING OF THE DAY...

Heavenly Father, May I have the courage today to say those words "I love you" with those that You have placed in my life. May my actions today, show them just how much I love them and thank You for the gift they bring to my life. AMEN.

Mark Dippre

October 19

ONE LESSON I HAVE LEARNED IN MY LIFE IS...

So much of life is not about what you do, but how you do it. I remember reading about the conversion of C.S. Lewis. He said, "Before I became a Christian I do not think I fully realized that one's life, after conversion, would inevitably consist in doing most of the same thing one had been doing before, one hopes in a new spirit, but still the same thing."

So today, I may do the same things I did yesterday. Only today, you and I can do them in a whole new way with a lot more meaning.

PRAYER FOR THE BLESSING OF THE DAY...

Lord God, give me a new heart and a new way to see life. Don't let me waste another day by keeping the same old attitude. I may not be able to change the world, but with Your help, Lord, I can put a whole new meaning on how I live my life. AMEN.

Fr. Dale

October 20

ONE LESSON I HAVE LEARNED IN MY LIFE IS...

A wise friend once told me that the key to understanding is to understand that there are some things that you will never understand. It really cleared things up for me!

PRAYER FOR THE BLESSING OF THE DAY...

(Psalm 46)

"Be still and know that I am God."

Kellie V.

October 21

ONE LESSON I HAVE LEARNED IN MY LIFE IS...

I am hungry for God. And the truth is, so are you. I think that is what unites us on a deeper level. We all have very different religious backgrounds. We come from different cultures, different parts of the country, and different political parties. Beyond all those differences is the human heart that longs for God and seeks God. The primary difference between spiritual people and non-spiritual people is that spiritual people admit their need and hunger for God. Non-spiritual people are still in denial. We all need a higher power that gives purpose to our lives and gives us strength when we are weak. Our hearts long for something, or someone, who is beyond this life.

PRAYER FOR THE BLESSING OF THE DAY...

The words from the song "Breathe" by Marie Barnett make a perfect prayer for today.

"And I'm desperate for You

"And I'm lost without You, Lord."

Fr. Dale

October 22

ONE LESSON I HAVE LEARNED IN MY LIFE IS...

We have all heard the saying, "it is better to give than to receive," and I have learned how true this statement really is.

Have you ever noticed how a simple act of kindness can change someone's life? Holding open a door, or being willing to carry a box for someone makes all the difference in the world. It shows that we care enough about the value of who they are. I remember in the seminary, we had service projects to help out the poor in our local community. One Saturday morning, our task was to cut and deliver wood before the cold Indiana winter set in, so that some local neighbors could be kept warm. We started out on that rainy freezing day with some less than enthusiastic classmates into the woods.

The day got colder the sleet came down faster. When we filled up the truck with wood, we found ourselves losing sight of what the mission was all about. That is, until we came to the first house and found a 91 year old woman named Grace who welcomed us with her smile. She never stopped saying the words "thank you, you made my day." As we unloaded her wood and filled up her stove to keep warm, she gave us all a hug and kiss. She said it was all that she could do, but wanted us to know that she was praying for us all that day. It was a very humbling experience for us to encounter, and I think that we received more that day than we gave. God showed us all how quickly it was better to "give rather than receive," for when we do so freely, he will reward us with a hug and a kiss of his love. Our attitudes changed in the weeks to come.

PRAYER FOR THE BLESSING OF THE DAY...

(Acts: 20:35)

"It is more blessed to give than to receive."

Heavenly Father, may I be generous with the gifts and talents You have blessed me with in my life, so that through my generosity, everyone I encounter today will know of Your LOVE. AMEN.

Mark Dippre

October 23

ONE LESSON I HAVE LEARNED IN MY LIFE IS...

That sometimes you do have to give in. I know the great Winston Churchill said "Never, never, never give up." And I believe that in general, that kind of determination is great. But, there are certain areas where reality is what it is.

I finally did give in and I joined AARP. You have to give AARP credit -- they have a very tenacious marketing program. And after awhile, for me, the reality set in that as long as I am getting older, a few discounts may help ease the blow.

Giving in is really not the same thing as giving up. Giving in is simply the realization that reality has changed. In accepting the new reality I can then begin to make the best of my current situation. I am aging. I don't have the energy I used to have. But I am alive, creative, and still very able to make a difference in the world and in the lives of other people.

Aging does change things. Realizing that is not all bad. But, as long as I am alive, my plan is to LIVE. I cannot give up on life nor can I accept that God no longer has a purpose for me in this world. And I trust, if that is true for me, it is true for you -- and for everyone.

PRAYER FOR THE BLESSING OF THE DAY...

Thank you, Lord for the precious gift of Life. May I always cherish it, and may I live each day to the fullest. AMEN.

Fr. Dale

October 24

ONE LESSON I HAVE LEARNED IN MY LIFE IS...

God gives each of us three birthdays. The first birthday is the day we enter the world. That's the day we all think of when we hear the word "birthday." It is a beautiful and wonderful expression of God's Love as He allows us to share in His creation. The second birthday is our baptism. It is the precious day God allows us to share in His world of grace. Our third birthday is the day we die in this world, but are born into eternity. That is the most important birthday of all. HEAVEN!

Now you may ask, "Why three?"

I believe it's God's favorite number, in honor of the Trinity: Birth in honor of the Father, Baptism in honor of the Spirit, and Heaven in honor of Jesus (Son). What a great God we have!

PRAYER FOR THE BLESSING OF THE DAY...

Lord, help me to appreciate the gift of my birth -- and the many births You give me. AMEN.

Fr. Dale

October 25

ONE LESSON I HAVE LEARNED IN LIFE IS...

If your sister or brother is also your ally, you have a bond that far exceeds being family. My sister Buffy was born on October 25, and my parents told me that she would be my friend forever. Those simple words defined who she was for me for the rest of my life. The greatest gift our parents ever gave us was each other.

PRAYER FOR THE BLESSING OF THE DAY...

Lord, bless my family members who are my friends, and my friends who have become my family members. May we always treat each other with respect, compassion, and as much good humor as can be mustered in any given situation.

Thank you, Lord, for the gift of friendship.

Jody Serey

October 26

ONE LESSON I HAVE LEARNED IN MY LIFE IS...

I don't like the idea of suffering. Or, maybe what I really don't like is the feeling of suffering. I'm sure most people don't like it!

Growing up, I was taught that suffering was good for the soul. I was told that our suffering completes the suffering of Jesus. What I was taught was wrong. The sacrifice and suffering of Jesus was perfect. I didn't need to add to it. I can't improve it.

Having said that, I do know there is value in sacrifice. The value is not in feeling pain, but rather in our own choice to give and do for others. Sacrifice has value when it comes from love, and it does something to help someone else.

Jesus did it all for us! And His call to us is to choose to love one another.

PRAYER FOR THE BLESSING OF THE DAY...

Thank you Jesus, for your perfect sacrifice on the cross. AMEN.

Fr. Dale

October 27

ONE LESSON I HAVE LEARNED IN MY LIFE IS...

"Don't sweat the small stuff."

Learn to observe, study, and dig for what is most important in each situation. Then concentrate on that.

As I concentrate on the important stuff, God has a way of taking care of the "small stuff" and the "big stuff."

[Luke 10:40 The Message (MSG)]

As they continued their travel, Jesus entered a village. A woman by the name of Martha welcomed him and made him feel quite at home. She had a sister, Mary, who sat before the Master, hanging on to every word he said. But Martha was pulled away by all she had to do in the kitchen. Later, she stepped in, interrupting them. "Master, don't You care that my sister has abandoned the kitchen to me? Tell her to lend me a hand."

PRAYER FOR THE BLESSING OF THE DAY...

Lord, help me to look at every situation through Your eyes. Your eyes show me what is important. Your eyes put everything in its rightful place. Help me to keep my eyes on You.

AMEN

Carol Taylor

October 28

ONE LESSON I HAVE LEARNED IN MY LIFE IS...

Never buy Halloween candy early. You think it will be there in the bowl when the big night arrives, but it will have disappeared like a ghost.

PRAYER FOR THE BLESSING OF THE DAY...

Lord, bless every child, every day, everywhere. You see each one, and know who is alone except for Your gaze upon a darkened face. Help bring the ones who need us into the light, and banish the shadows that protect us from seeing what the least of them among us endures.

Jody Serey

October 29

ONE LESSON I HAVE LEARNED IN MY LIFE IS...

I am not in control of outcomes. I am responsible for being open to guidance from the Spirit and for making myself available to do my part. But my part does not include choosing the outcome. It is like riding on a tandem bicycle with Jesus up front steering and I am on the back seat pedaling, providing control.

PRAYER FOR THE BLESSING OF THE DAY...

Lord, for so much of my adult life, I have tried to control outcomes. You have patiently taught me that "all is in divine order" even when "all" seems to be in disorder. I am thankful that all that occurs in my life is guided by You for my spiritual health and physical growth. I am Your son and I am grateful for Your continual love.

Greg Fyten

October 30

ONE LESSON I HAVE LEARNED IN MY LIFE IS...

I hate Halloween. I hate almost everything about it (except the candy). I hate the costumes, the skeletons, the horror movies, and most of all -- the ugly decorations.

The history of Halloween is interesting. It is actually part of the celebration of All Saints Day. Halloween was supposed to be a whimsical and scary way to get rid of evil spirits and clear the path to All Saints Day. Instead, in our culture, it has become a way to glorify evil. I am not saying we should not partake in Halloween. All I am saying is that for me, every year, it is a great reminder to pray evil away. No more violence, gun shootings, terrorism or fear. Let's work harder to simply glorify God.

PRAYER FOR THE BLESSING OF THE DAY...

Father, I pray today...

"Lead us not into temptation,

But deliver us from evil.

For Yours is the kingdom and the power, and the glory, forever and ever." AMEN.

Fr. Dale

October 31

ONE LESSON I HAVE LEARNED IN MY LIFE IS...

When I was almost 16, my parents sat down our already large family and said they had to talk to us one evening. I was anxious as I had a friend whose parents were divorcing and thought this had to be the news. Also, our Dad was an alcoholic which was difficult on our family. The news was, my mom was going to have another baby to add to our family of six kids! Four of us were teenagers; however, we took this news with great delight! (I later learned I should have been upset).

At 43 years old, and after a difficult pregnancy, my mom delivered a healthy baby sister to our family on Halloween evening. Little did we all know, we would all in so many different ways watch over our new sibling, Lisa. I always felt blessed and later learned my mom prayed constantly just to ask God for a healthy child. We were so blessed with her in our lives!

PRAYER FOR THE BLESSING OF THE DAY...

(Deuteronomy 7:13)

"He will love you, bless you, and multiply you. He will also bless the fruit of your womb and the fruit of your ground, your grain and your wine and your oil, the increase of your herds and the young of your flock, in the land that he swore to your fathers to give you."

Unexpected blessings are the best gifts of all. If your heart is open, many good things are given to you. We don't all know the good things that will come our way or what God has in store for us.

Praise and bless God for all of our blessings, as everything is a gift from God, even when it isn't expected!

Cindy A. Kiraly

November 1

ONE LESSON I HAVE LEARNED IN MY LIFE IS...

That when you say the word "saint" it often freaks out some Christians. And a feast day, like All Saints Day, especially makes them nervous. Many Christians feel like the saints detract from the centrality of Christ. And the truth is, over enthusiastic folks can seem to make the saints much more than they should be. But the word "saint" is actually a biblical term. It is used nearly 100 times from the Old Testament to the Book of Revelation. Paul uses it frequently to refer to Christians, martyrs, and all those who have been redeemed. So, no matter what religion you are part of, All Saints Day is a feast day for all of us to have been redeemed by Christ.

PRAYER FOR THE BLESSING OF THE DAY...

(Romans 12:9-13)

"Let love be genuine, hate what is evil, hold fast to what is good; love one another with mutual affection; outdo one another in showing honor. Do not lag in zeal, be ardent in spirit, serve the Lord. Rejoice in hope, be patient in suffering, persevere in prayer. Contribute to the needs of the saints: extend hospitality to strangers."

Fr. Dale

November 2

ONE LESSON I HAVE LEARNED IN MY LIFE IS...

That my reality is not in what I can see around me. My reality is in my faith in whom I can't see. My reality is in whom I know, through His Words, His Presence all around me, through me, and through those around me. God, You are my reality and truth.

[Acts 17:24-29 The Message (MSG)]

"The God who made the world and everything in it. This Master of sky and land, doesn't live in custom made shrines or need the human race to run errands for him, as if he couldn't take care of himself. He makes the creatures; the creatures don't make him. Starting from scratch, he made the entire human race and made the earth hospitable, with plenty of time and space for living so we could seek after God, and not just grope around in the dark but actually find him. He doesn't play hide-and-seek with us. He's not remote; he's near. We live and move in him, can't get away from him! One of the poets said it well: 'We're the God-created.' Well, if we are the God-created, it doesn't make a lot of sense to think we could hire a sculptor to chisel a god out of stone for us, does it?"

PRAYER FOR THE BLESSING OF THE DAY...

God of the Universe, God of all that is seen, thank you. Thank you that You designed me, You created me, You gave me life, and You have given me reality. Your unfathomable love is what gives me and creation truth and reality. AMEN.

Carol Taylor

November 3

ONE LESSON I HAVE LEARNED IN MY LIFE IS...

I need more courage. The word courage comes from the Latin word which means "heart". People who have heart inspire me to work harder, to face demons, and to stand for what is right and just. I want more heart. I want to live strong and imitate Jesus who had a heart filled with passion and love. I don't ever want to be afraid to think new, pray new, or love in a new way. The poet E.E. Cummings said, "It takes courage to grow up and become who you really are."

PRAYER FOR THE BLESSING OF THE DAY...

Lord, keep my blood pressure down and my passion pressure high. Let my heart be filled with courage as I face the issues of the day. Lord, do not let me grow weary, but keep me filled with passion and life.

Fr. Dale

November 4

ONE LESSON I HAVE LEARNED IN MY LIFE IS...

That when you are scared or anxious, in any situation, calling on the Holy Spirit will help ease your fears. It is truly amazing how the Holy Spirit works.

Lord Jesus, I desire to live in You, and for You to be alive in me. I know that I cannot do that without Your power. I accept/commit to You as Lord and Savior. Release in me the full power of Your Holy Spirit. With all my heart I say, "Come Holy Spirit, pour out Your gifts upon me."

PRAYER FOR THE BLESSING OF THE DAY...

(Acts 1:8)

"But you will receive power when the Holy Spirit has come upon you, and you will be my witnesses in Jerusalem and in all Judea and Samaria, and to the end of the earth."

Ned Trivanovich

November 5

ONE LESSON I HAVE LEARNED IN MY LIFE IS...

Letters are an endangered species all their own. There is something "alive" about a handwritten note, even if it is a hundred years old.

PRAYER FOR THE BLESSING OF THE DAY...

Lord, help me remember to keep some of the simple traditions that still mean so much in retrospect. Let me learn again the power of paper and pen, and a simple postage stamp. Don't let me become cynical about birthday cards and thank you notes, and the small gestures that keep us connected as family and friends. And when my words would have the power to comfort or heal, move me to write them down and place them in the hands of the one who needs to read them.

Jody Serey

November 6

ONE LESSON I HAVE LEARNED IN MY LIFE IS...

It is wise to plan our own funerals. If we do, we can at least control the choice of music and scripture readings. Beyond that, however, we will have no control over what people will say about us.

One of my favorite writers, and a friend of mine, Michael Yaconelli, wrote a book called Messy Spirituality. Yaconelli says, "Eulogies are delivered by people who know the deceased. I know what the consensus would be. Mike was a mess."

Mike wrote that in 2002. He died in an accident one year later.

So if you died today, what would be said about you? The truth is, by our own lives we are writing our eulogies day by day. By the way we treat others, love others, and serve others we are putting together the script for our funerals.

Mike Yaconelli saw himself as a "mess" and an imperfect Christian. But he never stopped trying to love and serve God. I think any of us would do well to be remembered the same way.

PRAYER FOR THE BLESSING OF THE DAY...

Heavenly Father, let me serve You with my whole heart today. Allow me to be an instrument of Your love for those I meet along the way. AMEN.

Fr. Dale

189

November 7

ONE LESSON I HAVE LEARNED IN MY LIFE IS...

Almost 50 percent of charitable giving is done during the months of October, November, and December. That's good because the need seems to be higher during the winter months and for Thanksgiving and Christmas. And it is good for all of us to get caught up in the season and in the wave of giving that happens.

I need to keep reminding myself, however, that giving all year round is a great privilege. To be blessed enough to be in a position to give is an honor and a responsibility. God expects me to simply be a good steward of the blessings I have received. I hope I can always honor Him by being generous, responsible, and grateful.

PRAYER FOR THE BLESSING OF THE DAY...

Gracious God,

You have generously poured Your blessings on me. Give me the grace I need to be a blessing to others.

Fr. Dale

November 8

ONE LESSON I HAVE LEARNED IN MY LIFE IS...

Wisdom is gained only after surviving a lot of stupid mistakes. Mistakes aren't fatal; failing to learn from mistakes can be deadly.

PRAYER FOR THE BLESSING OF THE DAY...

Lord, please forgive me for the arrogance of my youth, and the stubborn cynicism of my golden years. Overlook my pigheadedness, and claim me as Your own. I give You thanks for giving me the strength to rise up and walk, even when I have fallen so low that only Your eyes can see me.

Jody Serey

November 9

ONE LESSON I HAVE LEARNED IN MY LIFE IS...

The first part of November is when most elections take place. It's also a good time of year to remind ourselves to pray for new leaders. The word "politics" actually is not a bad word. It simply means the "art of human relationships." But in our country, it has become a bad word -- a harsh word, in fact.

Scripture sees leadership as a responsibility to God. Leaders will be held accountable to God as to how they used their power. Because of that, we must pray for leaders. Even if we don't agree with them or like them, they deserve our prayer support. We can't change them sometimes, but we can ask God to give them the grace they need to serve us well.

PRAYER FOR THE BLESSING OF THE DAY...

(1 Timothy 2:1-2)

"The first thing I want you to do is pray. Pray every way you know how, for everyone you know. Pray especially for rulers and their governments to rule well so we can be quietly about our business of living simply."

Fr. Dale

November 10

ONE LESSON I HAVE LEARNED IN MY LIFE IS...

Life dishes out hard days. When I am at the end of myself, when I have no control over circumstances, when there is nothing left but complete surrender -- I hang on by the skin of my teeth and a lot of faith. Life challenges have taught me that there is a greater purpose for my life no matter what events are unfolding around me. That is why I can hang on. Creation is a result of intelligent design, authored by God, for a higher purpose than I can ever know. Just look at the multitude of night stars following the same course, or the way a day is ordered by the sun and moon. There are no accidents. There is no coincidence. There is a great designer -- with a plan for each of us. How do I know? God's

Word tells me so. I have experienced it. He is the source and object of my faith and I trust Him.

Some people think the Bible is just human words written eons ago by men of their own accord, for their own intentions, not at all inspired. I know better. I know by faith that scripture is "God-breathed." My heart also knows it. There is truth in the breath of God. His truth never changes and it is always timely and applicable to whatever is happening in my life. I have come to depend on it for my survival.

Hearing God's word is easy. We all have ears to hear. But accepting God's word as TRUE is an act of faith. That's not so easy. Faith is a matter of the heart. It is not tangible. Faith transcends our human capacity for understanding, which is why it's sometimes so hard to grasp. When the evening stars disappear behind a cloudy night sky, does that mean they are no longer there? Is there reason to fear? Of course not! They are there! The clouds are just blocking them from sight. Faith is like that; it is not based on what I can see or touch. But rather, it anchors me to God in spite of what I see or don't see, and regardless of my circumstances.

PRAYER FOR THE BLESSING OF THE DAY...

Lord, thank You for the gift of faith. Thank you for life's challenges that have broken me to the point of surrender...where I find You waiting there for me. God, You are my strength, my hope, my comfort and my counsel. Help me to rest in that truth today. AMEN.

"Faith is the assurance of things hoped for, the conviction of things not seen." (Hebrews 11:1)

"For I know the plans that I have for You, declares the LORD, plans for welfare and not for calamity to give You a future and a hope." (Jeremiah 29:11)

Cheryl Armstrong

November 11

ONE LESSON I HAVE LEARNED IN MY LIFE IS...

Every day should be Veterans Day in this country. When President Woodrow Wilson declared November 11 to be a holiday, the primary intention was to set aside a day to reflect on the sacrifices of those who had served in the military during World War I. Observation of the holiday through parades and meetings was envisioned, and there was no question of gratitude on the part of the public.

We need to remember why our veterans often appear ragged and scarred, far beyond the scope of their physical wounds. We must not forget to express thanks to those who answered the call to duty. And when it becomes our turn to answer, we must never fail to protect the ones who protected us.

PRAYER FOR THE BLESSING OF THE DAY...

Lord, make me an instrument of Your peace. But do not let me belittle the sacrifices of those who gave the last full measure of their humanity to defend the peace we so often take for granted.

Lord, make me an instrument of Your peace. But help me bring peace of mind to the ones whose battle gear has been replaced with a cloak of despair.

Lord, make me an instrument of Your peace. But do not let me sink comfortably into complacency while our warriors wait in darkness for the rising of the sun.

Jody Serey

November 12

ONE LESSON I HAVE LEARNED IN MY LIFE IS...

That God is the Hound of Heaven. A poet named Francis Thompson wrote the famous poem by that name in the year 1893. Although it is a difficult poem to read, the point is clear. As the hound follows the rabbit, always coming closer and closer, so does God pursue us.

Most of us grow up in churches where we were told that we need to pursue God. But the truth is, God never stops seeking us. He desires an intimate relationship with us. And even though we pay no attention to God at times in our lives, He never gives up. We were created by God for God. His grace never gives up on us.

The fact that God is the Hound of Heaven is really good news. It's good news to the alcoholic who has struggled for decades. It's good news to the older person who fell away from God when they were in their twenties. It's good news for you and me knowing God will always, always seek us.

PRAYER FOR THE BLESSING OF THE DAY...

Thank you Jesus, for never giving up on any of us! AMEN.

Fr. Dale

November 13

ONE LESSON I HAVE LEARNED IN MY LIFE IS...

I want to avoid sin. Sin is just a nasty word...and sin itself is nastier. I don't want to be "sin-ister" in any way. What I have learned about avoiding sin is the best thing to do is to make an effort to do what is right and good.

In the old days people used to talk about the seven deadly sins. What's interesting is that each of these sins have "opposites." If I fill my life with the opposites, I don't have to worry about sin.

7 deadly sins are:	7 life giving opposites are:
Pride	Humility
Selfishness	Generosity
Lust	Purity
Anger	Meekness
Gluttony	Temperance
Envy	Love
Laziness	Diligence

When we fill our lives with love and positive virtues, we can crowd sin out of our lives. Life is like a shelf. We can fill it with worthless junk or use the space for valuable things.

PRAYER FOR THE BLESSING OF THE DAY...

(Philippians 4:8)

"Finally, brothers, whatever is true, whatever is honorable, whatever is just, whatever is pure, whatever is lovely, whatever is commendable, if there is any excellence, if there is anything worthy of praise, think about these things."

Fr. Dale

November 14

ONE LESSON I HAVE LEARNED IN MY LIFE IS...

Anything is possible; you just have to work for it and do things you've never done before. The more you give, the more you will get.

PRAYER FOR THE BLESSING OF THE DAY...

Lord, thank You for all You have given me and all I can share with others.

Janine Siegel

November 15

ONE LESSON I HAVE LEARNED IN MY LIFE IS...

To trust that the Lord will continue my daily reprieve from the desire to drink alcohol by guiding me in praising Him and doing His will to the best of my ability.

It was on Tuesday, November 13, 1974, that the Lord guided me to walk into my first Alcoholics Anonymous meeting which was held during the noon hour in the basement of an old church. I was trying to placate my wife who had made it very clear to me that she thought that I had a problem with alcohol and that AA could help me.

There were around 40 "old" men seated around a very long grouping of tables that welcomed me warmly and urged me to sit down and join them. I don't remember a lot about this first meeting other than it was smoky, which bothered me a bit since I had recently quit smoking,

Each of the men told me their story which brought them to Alcoholics Anonymous, which was the first step: they were powerless over alcohol and their lives had been unmanageable. They shared horrible stories: DUI convictions, jail terms, job firings, homelessness, car accidents killing innocent people, blackouts where they didn't know the women with whom they awoke the next morning, drinking alcohol first thing in the morning until they passed out, and a plethora of divorces and ruined relationships.

They urged me to do two things: cork the bottle and keep coming back. Because I trusted God, I did just that even though I had very serious doubts about being an alcoholic because none of those things they had talked about had happened to me. I didn't drink every day although when I did, I drank to get drunk. I hadn't lost or been fired from a job and didn't have any blackouts that I knew about nor did have any DUIs or kill anyone with my car.

I still had my doubts about being an alcoholic for at least another year until I came across the Second Edition of the Big Book which is called Alcoholics Anonymous. At that time, AA was using the Third Edition while today it's the Fourth Edition. In this Second Edition, there was an article entitled "The English Professor." All I had to do was change the word "English" to "Music," and there I was. No more denial; no more doubt! I had been fooling only myself!

It is now almost 31 years later, and the Lord blesses me daily. As long as I trust in Him, praise Him, and do His will to the very best of my ability, I continue to have the serenity of an alcohol free life as promised in the "Big Book" of Alcoholics Anonymous!

PRAYER FOR THE BLESSING OF THE DAY....

Nahum 1:7   The Lord is good; A stronghold in the day of trouble; and He knows those who trust in Him.

Reynold J. Krueger

November 16

ONE LESSON I HAVE LEARNED IN MY LIFE IS...

Be still and know! Sometimes it is difficult to have all of the faith and trust that brings us peace. Life can be so hard! It may seem that we are going through times and trials like no other, that there is no easy solution and that the problems of the world have never been as bad! The truth of the matter is: "There is nothing new under the sun" and "This, too, shall pass."

There are plenty of stories, even in the bible; that tell tales of wrong doing and despair that took place thousands of years ago, but the things that are happening now seem much more personal and real -- especially when they are happening to us, or those that we love.

We want answers. We want to be able to "fix it" now! It is at times like these when we need the support of someone that we trust, someone to simply be there with us through our struggle. When we hear phrases such as: "nothing new under the sun", and "this too shall pass", they can sound cold and uncaring -- especially when they come from the mouths of our family and friends. The struggles we are experiencing are personal. The feelings are strong, and the difficulties may seem insurmountable. At times like these we need to "Be still and know that God is in control."

God can, and will, make good come out of what seems to be bad. It may be hard to see or understand. We may learn what the positive is today, next week, or next year -- or we may never know. We have to have faith and trust that God is in to control, and everything happens exactly as it is supposed to. There are lessons to be learned. We need to learn them, be thankful for the lessons, and move on. Life is a gift. It must be lived; be thankful. You are loved!

PRAYER FOR THE BLESSING OF THE DAY...

Dear God, please help me to be still and know that You are in control. Help me to feel Your love every day in every situation. Help me to learn the lessons that I need in order to become the person that You wish for me to be. Give me Your compassion and love that I may share it with those who are suffering. Thank you for my life. Thank you for the lessons. Thank you for loving me. I love You. AMEN.

Kimberly Lynn O'Brien

November 17

ONE LESSON I HAVE LEARNED IN MY LIFE IS...

Sometimes the people and thoughts we fear become the same people and thoughts we hold so dear.

For many years I heard of the spiritual writings of ex-priest Brennan Manning. I was unwilling to read his stuff or learn about his teaching. Now, he is one of my favorite spiritual writers. He has amazing insight and spiritual depth.

In his book, All is Grace, Manning writes, "My message, unchanged for more than 50 years, is this: God loves you unconditionally, as you are and not as you should be, because nobody is as they should be. It is the message of grace."

I guess the real question is, why is such a simple message so hard for us to accept?

PRAYER FOR THE BLESSING OF THE DAY...

Lord, help me to see and accept Your truth... no matter who speaks it. Open my heart to Your spirit and Your Grace moving in places I least expect it.

Fr. Dale

November 18

ONE LESSON I HAVE LEARNED IN MY LIFE IS...

My favorite artist is Corita Kent. Corita was a nun, teacher, and artist. In the 1960s she designed posters and artwork revolving around peace and love. In fact, her most famous piece of art was her Love stamp produced in 1985. Her creative artwork used bright colors, sometimes symbols of modern culture, and powerful statements. My favorite Corita print was a very simple one that read, "I love you very." I purchased several posters and plates that had this quote on it. It was an easy way to say I love you to people.

It's time I find some new ways to express love. I used to say it 50 times a day. Now I say it from time to time. Saying "I love you" in posters, cards, or spoken words can change the world. At the very least it can change someone's day. As you read this, let me say "I love you very." And may you and I have courage to say these words frequently.

PRAYER FOR THE BLESSING OF THE DAY...

Lord, let me love with Your heart. And let me tell others I love them.

November 19

ONE LESSON I HAVE LEARNED IN MY LIFE IS...

A watched turkey never thaws.

PRAYER FOR THE BLESSING OF THE DAY...

Lord, help me remember the small tasks that add up to holiday celebrations. And help me sort through the "have tos" and the "shoulds" to arrive at what really has to be done.

Remind to find the joy in the mundane chores of potatoes and turkeys. Help me remember to share the work so that others can experience celebration in all its forms and phases.

It takes a village to raise a child, as the popular wisdom goes. It also takes a village to clean up after a holiday. Help me be grateful for the noise and the traffic in my kitchen, and remember the ones who are eating alone.

Jody Serey

November 20

ONE LESSON I HAVE LEARNED IN MY LIFE IS...

We should all take better care of our bodies. I read recently that babies being born today should plan to live to about 120 years of age. Many of us already grown adults will live to be 80 or 90 years old. Taking care of ourselves doesn't necessarily mean we will live a lot longer. It will mean that our life-quality will be better.

St. Francis of Assisi, the beloved saint from the early 1200s, made an interesting comment toward the end of his life. He said if he had one thing to do over, he would have treated "Brother Ass" a little better. Brother Ass is what Francis called his body. He worked hard, fasted, did penance, and walked hundreds of miles. Unlike Francis, I eat unhealthy foods, don't walk nearly enough, and get lazy when it comes to hard physical labor. But like Francis, if I am not careful, I will regret not being better to the body God gave me.

PRAYER FOR THE BLESSING OF THE DAY...

Heavenly Father, thank you for the gift of life. May I show my gratitude through self-care. AMEN.

Fr. Dale

November 21

ONE LESSON I HAVE LEARNED IN MY LIFE IS...

That true spirituality is hard in the United States. Spiritual writer Richard Rohr says that what is most exciting to Americans is either success or gathering more material possessions. Rohr says that American Christians have "more of a spirituality of taking instead of giving." Americans want to take something away from church that makes them feel better about their lives. And week after week, many of us want the church to give us a spiritual or emotional high.

Rohr is right. True spirituality is not about taking, it is about surrendering to God. In the very act of giving ourselves to God and surrendering to His will, the spiritual life begins. Letting go of control and our need for more stuff is the only way that true spirituality and the Gospel can be lived!

PRAYER FOR THE BLESSING OF THE DAY...

Lord, help me to surrender to You. Give me the courage and strength to let go of control and begin to live as a true disciple. AMEN.

Fr. Dale

November 22

ONE LESSON I HAVE LEARNED IN MY LIFE IS...

That fear of the unknown is an emotionally crippling behavior. Being afraid of what might happen creates problems that don't exist. I have wasted too much time and emotional energy on fear of the unknown – "what might happen." Not only is this behavior damaging to me, it screams loud and clear that I am not trusting God and His power to take care of me.

[Ephesians 6:13-18 The Message (MSG)]

200

Be prepared. You're up against far more than you can handle on your own. Take all the help you can get, every weapon God has issued, so that when it's all over but the shouting you'll still be on your feet. Truth, righteousness, peace, faith, and salvation are more than words. Learn how to apply them. You'll need them throughout your life. God's Word is an indispensable weapon. In the same way, prayer is essential in this ongoing warfare. Pray had and long. Pray for your brothers and sisters. Keep your eyes open. Keep each other's spirits up so that no one falls behind or drops out.

PRAYER FOR THE BLESSING OF THE DAY...

Lord, thank You. You are in charge of my now and my future. I put my life in Your Hands. You keep me safe and whole. You are my safe haven. Thank you. AMEN.

Carol Taylor

November 23

ONE LESSON I HAVE LEARNED IN MY LIFE IS...

Unless somebody in the family brings home a food stylist for the holidays, my table is not going to be worthy of photos no matter how many cute little decorations I scatter around it.

PRAYER FOR THE BLESSING OF THE DAY...

Lord, please make everything edible even if my dinners aren't picturesque. Let the conversation be lively and warm, and the emphasis be on the faces gathered together to share so much more than a meal.

And if I am alone, let me give thanks for memories and the glow of love remembered. For when You are with me, there is feasting and celebration.

Jody Serey

November 24

ONE LESSON I HAVE LEARNED IN MY LIFE IS...

"I can do all thing with Christ who strengths me." (Philippians 4:13)

Yes. That is Paul talking. But, not ALL things should be done by me.

A huge lesson that I was privileged to learn was at the hands of a special friend mired in the misery of an alcoholic spouse. She could not drive at night and I offered take her to AA meetings. I was a young adult, free of family responsibilities, not working, and I thought there was nothing in life that I couldn't do something about. I wanted to help.

The Serenity Prayer starts with "Lord, give me serenity to accept the things I cannot change..." Do You, Lord, mean there are things I cannot do? There are things I must "let go, and let God"? What might that be?

I spent two and half years learning the wisdom to know the difference. I can change me. I cannot change anyone else.

PRAYER FOR THE BLESSING OF THE DAY...

Lord, please let me never lose sight of that basic lesson. Help me to be humble and to know Your way is best.

Jean Bruno

November 25

ONE LESSON I HAVE LEARNED IN MY LIFE IS...

That the word generosity comes from the same word as "genes" in Latin genus. It means we share the same "genes" or "stock" as someone else. And because we are "connected" with someone else we give to them liberally.

When God took on human flesh in the person of Jesus, we started sharing "genes" with God. And although God is generous by nature, in Jesus He gives us life, mercy, grace, and blessings in ABUNDANCE. What a great and generous God we have!

PRAYER FOR THE BLESSING OF THE DAY...

Lord, help me to imitate You today. Give me a thankful spirit always ready to share my blessings with others. Thank you, Lord, for being so ABUNDANT with me.

Fr. Dale

November 26

ONE LESSON I HAVE LEARNED IN MY LIFE IS...

I don't really care for the inspirational piece about footprints in the sand. It tells of a single set of footprints appearing in the sand when God was carrying the person, and were not the result of the person walking alone as the person suspected.

I'm sure this piece provides solace for many others, and I am not diminishing that possibility. It's just that if there were footprints in the sand left by God and me, mine would be the drag marks that went all the way down the beach as He hauled me along to where I needed to go.

PRAYER FOR THE BLESSING OF THE DAY...

Lord, understand that my reluctance to step into the fray is not because I don't want to follow You. It's more often because I'm aware of my limitations, and just how ineffectual my efforts can seem sometimes.

If You want to me act, don't let me rest. If You want me to speak, don't let me stay silent. This servant's heart beats because You gave it life. And the life You gave it is Yours alone to claim.

Jody Serey

November 27

ONE LESSON I HAVE LEARNED IN MY LIFE IS...

We all need a code of ethics to live by. That code becomes the prism through which we see the world and decide how we will choose to behave. After many years of thinking, acting, messing up, and reflecting, I finally know what mine is; it is simply "honor God." In all I do and say, that's what I want to do! I want to make sure I honor God in the way I speak, in my commitment to allow Him to judge others, and in the way I see others. I guess part of the reason I want to share this with you is to invite you to "honor God" with me.

PRAYER FOR THE BLESSING OF THE DAY...

God, I choose to love You, with all my heart, all my soul, and all my being! May I be faithful to my commitment to You. AMEN.

Fr. Dale

November 28

ONE LESSON I HAVE LEARNED IN MY LIFE IS...

I have learned the importance of the family unit. For as long as I can remember when growing up in an Italian neighborhood in Chicago in the '50s, every activity was family based. We weren't the exception; we were the norm. Families worshipped together, ate meals together, vacationed together, all while building lasting bonds of trust and love.

What's happened to mankind over the last 50 years? Over time we've become a society so fast-paced, so competitive, and so impersonal that our treasured values have tarnished and lost their meaning.

Young people today are lucky if they have two loving parents living under the same roof. Because each modern day family member has their own agenda, circle of friends, interests and activities, they often don't make time for worship, family meals or even talking.

PRAYER FOR THE BLESSING OF THE DAY...

Lord, help us all reconnect, redefine and enrich the family unit as You created it to be. Let our children and future generations experience Your unconditional love and come to know and witness a secure family bond as I did, not so many years ago.

Strengthen our faith and trust in You, Heavenly Father. Bring peace and joy to the fallen and hope for us all.

Thomas Cutrera

November 29
ONE LESSON I HAVE LEARNED IN MY LIFE IS...

By late November, I am often tempted to check off the rest of this year and pin my hopes on the upcoming New Year. This is not a good thing.

PRAYER FOR THE BLESSING OF THE DAY...

Lord, keep me from wishing my life away. Please strike the words "I can't wait until it's over" from my speech, and replace them with "I'm glad I'm here right now."

Help me feel truly blessed to find my feet moving through another day. Remind me that my steps are always taken in companionship with You, and that the one scuffing their feet is never You.

Jody Serey

November 30

ONE LESSON I HAVE LEARNED IN MY LIFE IS...

There is never enough time. I don't mean time to clean the dust bunnies from under the bed or tidying up when company's coming.

The time I'm speaking of is the time we spend with the people God has placed in our lives. The memories we've made coloring with a child or having lunch with an old friend. The times when we have really been present, listening and laughing with those we cherish.

Scripture tells us that Jesus made time to be with His friends. Can we have a better example?

PRAYER FOR THE BLESSING OF THE DAY...

Loving God, help us to realize the importance of prioritizing our time and giving our loved ones the attention they deserve. In Jesus' name, we pray. AMEN.

(Scripture: Luke 10:38-42)

Betty Clewell

December 1

ONE LESSON I HAVE LEARNED IN MY LIFE IS...

That as we get older, years seem to pass more quickly. Here we are in December once again. It is time to start RAMPING up for Christmas.

I know one thing about this Christmas. I don't want to waste it! Many Christmases have come and gone without much spiritual growth. I really don't want another cookie-filled, shopping-filled, party-filled, thing-filled Christmas season. I want a real Christ-"mas" -- which in Spanish means "more Jesus." And I also know, that if I don't do something to make it more spiritual, that I will AGAIN get distracted by things that don't matter.

PRAYER FOR THE BLESSING OF THE DAY...

Lord, open my heart to You. I want You more deeply in my life. As we all prepare for Your faith, let my preparation be more spiritual than ever. Remind me to do something for the poor, to pray with more sincerity and intensity, and help me to see You every moment of my life. AMEN.

Fr. Dale

December 2

ONE LESSON I HAVE LEARNED IN MY LIFE IS...

My quote "December is the toughest month of the year. Others are July, January, September, April, November, May, March, June, October, August, and February". Unquote. Mark Twain said that and he hit the nail on the head, as far as I'm concerned. But December truly is a month that tests my perseverance more than the other eleven on the calendar. As the Christmas season (or holiday season, ugh) begins, retailers have a bad habit of beginning Christmas in November or even October in search of the almighty dollar. If I had my way the people of the world would remember to put CHRIST back in Christmas.

PRAYER FOR THE BLESSING OF THE DAY...

Lord of all, You are a God of plenty, a Lord who provides for us in our need As I begin these early days of Advent, help me to believe that You know what I need. Give me the courage to listen to Your voice and the freedom to open my heart to the graces You are offering me to place my trust in You. And show the world how to have a deeper faith in You.

(1 Timothy 6:10)

Weldon Turner

December 3

ONE LESSON I HAVE LEARNED IN MY LIFE IS...

Is that this is one of the most beautiful times of the year. Not because of the weather (cold and sunny in the East, sunny and wonderful in Arizona) but because of what we are doing as Christians. The whole Christian world is celebrating Advent. The word "Advent" is a Latin word which means "to come." We are waiting for the coming of Christ at Christmas, that amazing event when God became one of us. Even beyond that, we are waiting for the second coming of Christ at the end of the world. That, too, like Christmas, will be a glorious day.

There is a lot to do in Advent. Gifts to buy. Cookies to bake. Cards to send. But, beyond all that, Advent is supposed to be the time we heighten our senses to watch for the daily coming of Christ into our lives. There are so many ways that the Lord comes into our lives each day: our family, the needy, the events of life, and the whispers of the Holy Spirit. If we can get in tune with these "comings,", it would change our lives and our attitudes.

Today, tomorrow, and the next day will be busy. But, if we are actively looking to see God in our world, we can have the best Advent season ever. And, I promise, it will make our Christmas celebration much more spiritual and joyful.

PRAYER FOR THE BLESSING OF THE DAY...

We bless You, God our Father, for this time of Advent that Your love offers to us.

We pray to You:

Prepare in the desert of our heart the path of return to Your Son Jesus.

The hills of our pride - bring low by Your humility.

The valleys of our despair - fill with Your hope.

The twisted paths of our lies - straighten through Your truth joy bloom in our desert.

Then we will be able to celebrate the glory of Your love and worship Your salvation, Your Son Jesus, our Savior. AMEN.

Fr. Dale

December 4

ONE LESSON I HAVE LEARNED IN MY LIFE IS...

Today, December 4, is National "pray for those we love day." By the way, I declared it to be that day! And why not? There is no better day than today to pray for family and friends.

One of the greatest gifts we can give is the gift of prayers. Prayer isn't the kind of gift that can be wrapped in a bow or put in a gift bag. Prayer is our asking God to cover those we love with His mantel of grace. Prayer is asking God to give our loved ones the grace and strength they need to make good choices and to have a good life.

The truth is that some people in our lives need a lot of prayer. And they need prayers for a long time. We can't give up on them. No sickness, no addiction, no human situation is more powerful than God. The bible tells us to be like the woman who kept going to the judge. That kind of persistence is needed.

PRAYER FOR THE BLESSING OF THE DAY...

Father, I ask Your blessing on those that I hold most dear in my heart. Surround my family and friends with Your unconditional love. I pray especially for (names)_____. AMEN.

Fr. Dale

December 5

ONE LESSON I HAVE LEARNED IN MY LIFE IS...

We do not do enough to help others throughout the world. I love our country and I know we need to do more to help our own countrymen. There are sure a lot of needs in our neighborhood, city, state, and country. But we also need to think beyond our borders. It is not enough to help our own.

The important thing about giving to missions or other countries is that we receive nothing in return. We don't see or experience the results. But in feeding others throughout the world, we are acknowledging that we know Jesus is in each person. When we care for someone far away, we are caring for Jesus. In fact, what a great Christmas gift to give

Jesus -- feeding Him in a faraway place.

PRAYER FOR THE BLESSING OF THE DAY...

Father, help me to see the presence of Your son in each person who lives in our world. Give me a desire to care for Your son, in caring for the poorest of the poor.

Fr. Dale

December 6

ONE LESSON I HAVE LEARNED IN MY LIFE IS...

Christmas is my favorite time of year. I love that everywhere you look there are signs of the holiday. I know it drives some people crazy that Christmas decorations are out by the time fall hits. And I must admit, I am one of the people guilty of putting a tree up long before Thanksgiving. But, I love my tree and I love what it stands for. But, you have to understand, that in my small condo I have a collection of over 50 crosses. Maybe it's just me, but the more aware I am of God, the better chance I have of being faithful. I need all the help I can get.

I know Christianity is not about externals. Rather, it is about changing our hearts. But because we are human, physical reminders of faith can help us to make good daily decisions to follow Christ. I pray that all the nativities, trees, lights, and stars we see this Christmas season remind us that Jesus Christ is the light of the world and the light of our lives.

PRAYER FOR THE BLESSING OF THE DAY...

(John 1: 3-5)

"Through him all things came into being, not one thing came into being without him. What has come into being was life, life that was the light of men, and light shines in the darkness, and darkness could not overpower it."

Fr. Dale

December 7

ONE LESSON I HAVE LEARNED IN MY LIFE IS...

Sometimes going on with ordinary life in extraordinary times is an act of bravery in itself. My mother talked about how difficult it was to put up the Christmas tree after the bombing of Pearl Harbor in 1941. She said her family knew that the world had changed forever, and they were also sure that many young men would go to war and not come home again.

But they put up the tree, and they hung the decorations as they always did every year. Mom said, "We knew that life would go on, and we would always find a way to celebrate Christmas – no matter what."

PRAYER FOR THE BLESSING OF THE DAY...

Lord, help me set aside pain and worry to allow the goodness of life to reach me. If I am blinded by my own tears, make me see that the same sun that disappears at night also rises in the morning. Do not let me fall prey to despair and doubt, and help me stand up and walk when I would rather lie still forever.

Jody Serey

December 8

ONE LESSON I HAVE LEARNED IN MY LIFE IS...

Memories are not always accurate. I remember the verse, John 3:16, "For God so loved the world He gave his only Son so that anyone who believes in him shall not perish but have eternal life." My husband remembers that the verse was Romans 10:9, "For if you tell others with your own mouth that Jesus Christ is your Lord, and believe in your own heart that God has raised him from the dead, you will be saved."

Either John 3:16 or Romans 10:9 was on the transom of a sailboat that we followed into a safe harbor in the Georgian Bay. We got to know the owners of that sailboat. If and only if you asked them why they named their boat with a biblical verse, they told their story. The wife had been very ill and the husband had vowed to proclaim his loyalty to God if she recovered.

Nice story? Yes. But also it is the most effective and least objectionable demonstration of evangelization I have ever seen.

I don't want somebody to tell me what they believe in the manner that suggests, "I am right; you are wrong." But am curious about how a person comes to believe what they do believe. If I had been Chinese, just what in the Christian message would make sense? If my heritage was tribal Africa, why would I choose Christianity? What part of Christianity isn't in any other religion?

PRAYER FOR THE BLESSING OF THE DAY...

Dear Father, thank you for my faith. Thank you for my belief there is a God and I am not it. Jesus, knowing that You walked this earth and dealt with adversity is comforting. Learning by Your example to treat others as would want people to treat me seems to be a self-evident truth. I am simply and completely grateful.

Jean Bruno

December 9

ONE LESSON I HAVE LEARNED IN MY LIFE IS...

One of the best scripture quotes comes from St. Paul in the letter to the Philippians. Paul says, "I can do all things through him who strengthens me." (4:13)

What that means to me is that even when I think I do not have the strength or the ability to make it through something, that the strength of Christ can carry me through. This saying became very important to me during the darkest days of my life. I found I was able to keep standing in Christ even though I had been knocked down so many times. In Christ, we can bear any trial, perform any duty, and fight any evil.

PRAYER FOR THE BLESSING OF THE DAY...

Jesus, You are my strength when I am weak. Your grace will always be enough for me to do whatever You ask of me. AMEN.

Fr. Dale

December 10

ONE LESSON I HAVE LEARNED IN MY LIFE IS...

Images stay with us. We remember meaning and significance when we make an image out of words. In Acts 7:54 Stephen, when he was being stoned, "...gazed steadily upward into heaven and saw the glory of God and Jesus standing at the right hand of God." (Life Application Bible)

Usually Jesus is described as sitting at the right hand of God. In this case, His standing suggests He will be presenting Stephen's soul to God much like a lawyer does in a court room defending his client.

This story came to mind having heard our daughter tell her son about college life. "You don't have to do homework, you don't even have to attend class, and you just have to pass the tests... But, (a long pause for emphasis), don't ask that professor for a letter of recommendation." College is about learning how to learn so that you can teach yourself what you will need to know. It will take practice and a concerted effort.

PRAYER FOR THE BLESSING OF THE DAY...

Thank you, dear Jesus, for encouraging me to be diligent, to not give up when things are tough. Thank you for teaching me to keep learning. Thank you for helping me to appreciate that life is no tougher for me than anyone else. My soul bounds in joy knowing You are with me every step of the way.

Jean Bruno

December 11

ONE LESSON I HAVE LEARNED IN MY LIFE IS...

Christmas is all about giving. I know that the greatest feeling is planning and doing something special for someone else. There is a real joy in going overboard for someone else. By making someone else feel special, we can begin to understand the meaning of Christmas.

I know God is not human and He doesn't have human emotions. But, I can't help myself as I imagine the excitement God felt right before that first Christmas. He knew He was going to surprise humanity and give us the greatest gift EVER. In fact, He was so excited that even the angels were singing.

There is still time to do something very loving and very generous this Christmas. I think we should all get to work and start planning.

PRAYER FOR THE BLESSING OF THE DAY...

Lord, make this the best Christmas ever for my family. Give me a generous heart... and excitement about giving. AMEN.

Fr. Dale

December 12

ONE LESSON I HAVE LEARNED IN MY LIFE IS...

Joy is an important part of the Christian life. I remember hearing a preacher say, "Joy is no laughing matter." I thought it was not so insightful saying joy should involve an outward expression like laughing or smiling. But the preacher was right in saying it is much deeper than that. For Christians, joy is one of the fruits of the Holy Spirit. Joy is the ability to delight in God. Joy allows us to experience a deeper sense of gladness and happiness no matter what the events are in our lives. Joy is a tremendous gift from God. I pray for it for myself and for you.

PRAYER FOR THE BLESSING OF THE DAY...

Psalm 47

> "Clap your hands, all you peoples;
>
> shout to God with loud songs of Joy.
>
> For the Lord, the Most High, is
>
> awesome,
>
> He is a great king over all the earth."

Fr. Dale

December 13

ONE LESSON I HAVE LEARNED IN MY LIFE IS...

It is important for the giver of a gift to find a recipient. Giving and receiving are two parts of the same process. Gifts become treasures when they leave loving hands and are placed into ones that welcome them.

PRAYER FOR THE BLESSING OF THE DAY...

Lord, in this season of giving, let me offer up what is truly mine to give. Let whatever I give to another be of me, and not just from me.

Jody Serey

December 14

ONE LESSON I HAVE LEARNED IN MY LIFE IS...

I adore their smiles. I cherish their hugs. I admire their hearts -- but most of I love that I have children that love me. Sometimes the bad things that happen in our lives put us directly on the path to the best things that will ever happen to us. Those memories will always be with me and will cherished forever.

I chose this day to write a devotional because it is the birthday of my last daughter. She has been going through some difficult times, but always has smile on her face and knows that God will always be there for her. And now she is going to be grandmother and I hope she has as much love in her heart as I had raising my children.

PRAYER FOR THE BLESSING OF THE DAY...

All it takes is one song to bring back a thousand memories. Lord, please be the music that my heart longs to hear.

Janet Eicher

December 15

ONE LESSON I HAVE LEARNED IN MY LIFE IS...

Jesus Christ is amazing. The miracles he worked, the lessons he taught, and the salvation he gave us are far beyond anything any other human being has done. Why is this so important? Because it is time we start proclaiming Jesus with a lot more enthusiasm and life. Jesus was not the founder of a boring religion filled with rituals and rules. He came to show us how to live life to the fullest. He brought joy and hope to people of every race, generation, and status. He changed the world forever by calling others to love and forgive. He rose from the dead and conquered our greatest human fear -- death. And yes, Jesus was not only fully human he was 100 percent fully God. And, by coming and living in our midst he raised up all of humanity to a new level of dignity. It's worth it to take time to learn more about the life and message of Jesus. And, as we do, we will learn the greatest story ever told, about the greatest person who ever lived. And, that, my friends, is AMAZING.

PRAYER FOR THE BLESSING OF THE DAY...

Isaiah 7:14

All right then, the Lord himself will give you the sign. Look! The virgin will conceive a child. She will give birth to a son and will call him Emmanuel, which means "God is with us."

Thank you, Lord, for the incredible gift of Your Son, Jesus. May I always follow Him with enthusiasm and love. AMEN.

Fr. Dale

December 16

ONE LESSON I HAVE LEARNED IN MY LIFE IS...

A Beethoven's birthday reflection:

Music is such an important element in our praise and worship! I deeply value the blessing of sung prayer provided by so many gifted composers and musicians over the years. Take a moment to reflect on how they've supported our communal responsibility, to give attention and participation in prayer. I hope that you share my appreciation for all whose poetic and melodic gifts assist our hearts to pray and give praise.

I'm humbly grateful for the different opportunities I've had to play with some fine liturgical musicians. Tom Booth recently reminded a bunch of us of the 30th anniversary of the first Life Teen Mass! Over twenty years ago, I was at a large conference at North American Liturgy Resources in Phoenix. Sitting next to Michael Joncas, who'd I'd known from earlier days in Minnesota, I said, "Well, I'm just an amateur here today."

I've never forgotten his response, "Well, Terry, you know what that term means? 'Lover of _____'!"

Being a part of a group that collaborates to prepare for the worship of a purposed community, whether sharing joy or love, or even lament, has been an awesomely happy responsibility. I've seen the power of a song to carry our prayer outside the confines of mere words into a holier, freer space. I've also rejoiced over the subliminal power of using "we", "us", or "our", rather than singular pronouns in lyrics.

And I praise some really strong lyrics that invade our heads, and hearts, so that we continue to carry that prayer into the other parts of our lives. Some truly bold statements in a song keep us focused on a call to justice, compassion, and healing. Think of a recent example we've sung: "As for me in my house / We will serve the Lord! / We have builded...".

I decided to share below one quietly comforting prayer/song from the album Picture the Dawning that frequently plays in my heart, ever since I first heard it 40 years ago. I often add "You" after "Lord" and at the beginning of each statement, and refocus my prayer on praise and thanksgiving for God's grace and mercy. Since I can't include the tune, here's a link to the original recording:

http://j.mp/spreadyourlove

PRAYER FOR THE BLESSING OF THE DAY...

"Lord, look upon the face of Your servant. Heed my cry for help;

Heed my cry for strength and courage and peace.

Lord, look upon Your children in Your kindness

See how we reach out; See how much we need Your strength and love.

Lord, Lord, Lord, Look upon us, Never turn away; Heal us, Lord.

Lord, transform our hearts; Fill us with pow'r to spread Your peace and love.

Spread Your love."

Terry J Bolduc

December 17

ONE LESSON I HAVE LEARNED IN MY LIFE IS...

You can never predict the future. We plan. We hope. We manipulate things to go our way. But none of these mean that life will go the way we think.

Some folks have a harder time with the unknown than others. All the Type "A" personalities reading this hate hearing they can't plan enough to insure the outcome they want. But, the truth is, other people change their minds, the weather changes on a whim, and we do not have the ability or strength to make everyone do the right thing.

So -- does that mean we give up and simply don't plan or work out to make things happen? No; we give it our best shot. But, we should never be taken by surprise when the unknown happens. When we expect the unexpected, life doesn't get so traumatic. After all, in the end, God never abandons us. And even if we end up on an unknown road, He has paved a way for us.

PRAYER FOR THE BLESSING OF THE DAY...

Lord, God, You are worthy of my trust. I know You love me, and I know You are with me. Grant me a sense of peace, even when I do not know where life is leading me. AMEN.

Fr. Dale

December 18

ONE LESSON I HAVE LEARNED IN MY LIFE IS...

This time of the year is very stressful: not enough time to get the holiday things done, it is getting too expensive, the advertising is over the top ; oh my, what do I get my wife this year?

I have learned that the world pushes and pulls us in so many directions – and Jesus gets lost in the whole holiday chaos.

So, I have also learned to take a deep breath, slow down, refocus and prepare the way for the celebration of the coming of salvation. I relook at the relationships I have developed over the years. Am I a good friend? Do I love unselfishly? Am I supporting my church both in prayer and financially? Do I show unfettered appreciation to those who serve in our community? Am I truly imitating Jesus on a daily basis?

PRAYER FOR THE BLESSING OF THE DAY...

Father God, thank you for the gift of Your only Son and the salvation He brought to us. Let me see the miraculous star that points me to Jesus every day. Thank you for being the Father I can count on and lean on. Let us all see the true meaning of Christmas as we approach that day of celebration . I love You, Lord!

(Proverbs 4:23-27)

John Null

December 19

ONE LESSON I HAVE LEARNED IN MY LIFE IS...

The longer the Christmas newsletter, the more the writer isn't saying.

PRAYER FOR THE BLESSING OF THE DAY...

Lord, help me to avoid being jealous of other people's seemingly perfect lives, while mine lies in a messy tangle like old tinsel. Remind me that everybody is wrestling pain and sorrow that nobody knows about, and I should not presume that my own circumstances are less desirable than another's. Nudge me when I'm tempted to fall prey to envy. Jostle me when I look with a critical eye at my own blessings.

Jody Serey

December 20

ONE LESSON I HAVE LEARNED IN MY LIFE IS...

Sometimes, a picture is worth a thousand words. In my memory there is a picture painted by a Spanish artist of Paul lying on the ground beside a horse. It appears he fell off the horse. The reference is to a scene described in Acts 9:4: "As he was nearing Damascus on this mission, suddenly a brilliant light from heaven spotted down upon him! He fell to the ground and heard a voice saying to him 'Paul, Paul! Why are you persecuting me?'" (Life Application Bible)

I asked my pastor about the apparent discrepancy between the painting and the words. He quipped, "Perhaps Paul fell off his high horse."

Oh, yes, we do ride the horse telling God what we want.

We cringe when we have to say "Thy will be done."

I remember wanting to go roller-skating, but my parents said "no." I knew at the age of 10 there was no use in begging, whining, negotiating, saying "but everybody else is going." No meant no! When I had a child of my own, I was grateful for having learned that lesson early. Consequently, life in my household was always more peaceful.

PRAYER FOR THE BLESSING OF THE DAY...

Dear Lord, thank you for all the lessons You have taught me; thank you for the teachers who loved their jobs; thank you for the myriad good and bad experiences that have given me wisdom; thank you for my parents who did their best, thank you for my children who continue to teach me how hard it is to do the right thing; thank you for my friends who love to learn; thank you for the humility to accept the world as I find it and not as I want it. AMEN.

Jean Bruno

December 21

ONE LESSON I HAVE LEARNED IN MY LIFE IS...

We all need grace. What do we know about grace? First, it's more than a song ("Amazing Grace"). It is the very life of God working in us. He works at times and in places we don't understand. But, He continues to make miracles happens in the most unlikely places with the most unlikely folks.

Episcopal priest Robert Farrar Capon wrote, "In Jesus, God has put a 'gone fishing' sign on the religion shop. He has done the whole job in Jesus once and for all and simply invited us to believe it – to trust the organic proposition that in him, every last person on earth is already home free without a single religious exercise. It's crazy. It's weird, outrageous, and vulgar."

Wow – "vulgar grace." Now that is new insight!

PRAYER FOR THE BLESSING OF THE DAY...

"Amazing Grace, how sweet the sound
That saved a wretch like me.
I once was lost, but now I am found.
Was blind, but now I see."

Fr. Dale

December 22

ONE LESSON I HAVE LEARNED IN MY LIFE IS...

That Jesus is Emmanuel, that is, "God with us." That is a very strong statement about God -- that He "is with us."

To any of us who have gone through difficult times in our lives, we know the importance of having someone "with us." Being alone is one of the greatest fears any human being experiences. Dying alone is frightening. Being alone in a hospital in a city where we don't know anyone is difficult. To me, even thinking about being totally alone in a time of crisis is hard. In my own life, going through several years of isolation was almost overwhelming. The very few people who were with me were life savers to me.

If Jesus is Emmanuel, then we are never alone. No matter where the events of life lead us, God goes with us -- in fact, He goes before us.

We have so much to celebrate this Christmas. We celebrate family, friends, love, hope, and another new beginning. But most important, we celebrate "God-with-us."

PRAYER FOR THE BLESSING OF THE DAY...

Come, Lord! Come! Make this the most beautiful and spiritual Nativity ever! AMEN.

Fr. Dale

December 22

ONE LESSON I HAVE LEARNED IN MY LIFE IS...

No family is perfect, no family get together is perfect, no photo of a family get together is perfect. But it can all be perfectly wonderful if we don't demand perfection.

PRAYER FOR THE BLESSING OF THE DAY...

Lord, help me keep it real. Focus my heart on the things that matter. Remind me that all the tinsel and silver bells cannot muffle the small, thin cry of a child on top of hay in a manger.

Drive me to my knees with the majesty of the perfect gift the world was given, created out of perfect love.

Jody Serey

December 23

ONE LESSON I HAVE LEARNED IN MY LIFE IS...

I have learned not to waste Christmas. Tomorrow is Christmas Eve already. In the course of life we only get 70, 80, or maybe 90 of these. It seems that Christmas in the first third of life is magical and meaningful. The second third of life means Christmas is a lot of work trying to make the day special for others. In the last third of life, we somehow become spectators at Christmas. We go to church, eat well, and watch others enjoy it. But it doesn't need to become faded for us. We can still make memories. We can still show love. We can give, serve, sing louder at service, blow someone away with kindness, we can pray more intently than ever. We can make this Christmas one of the best ever.

PRAYER FOR THE BLESSING OF THE DAY...

Jesus, give me a heart filled with passion and love for You. Let me celebrate Your birth in a new and deeper way. AMEN.

Fr. Dale

December 24

ONE LESSON I HAVE LEARNED IN MY LIFE IS...

Very few people go to church on Christmas Day anymore. Almost everyone goes Christmas Eve. Some folks think it's more convenient to go on Christmas Eve. Others want a quiet Christmas morning. The truth is -- it really doesn't matter when you go. No one knows what day Jesus was really born, anyway. The more important thing is to let the message of Christmas come into our hearts. Today, we celebrate God becoming one of us. No other religion in the world claims such a thing. That is what makes Christianity "good news!" Celebrate today, tonight, tomorrow, and always -- the good news that God is with us!

PRAYER FOR THE BLESSING OF THE DAY...

Heavenly Father,

We praise You for Your Son, Jesus. He is Emmanuel, the hope of all people, May He be born today into my heart in a new and deeper way. May His light fill the darkness in our world. AMEN.

Fr. Dale

December 25

ONE LESSON I HAVE LEARNED IN MY LIFE IS...

Christmas is one of the BEST days of the year. I know it can be a painful day for some. Anyone who has lost a loved one in the past year struggles. And, those who have a family member deployed in the military find holes in their hearts. Many folks in financial trouble suffer a lot as well. But still, Christmas brings hope.

The central message of Christmas is Emmanuel, God-is-with-us. No other religion can claim that their God loved them so much that God Himself came to be in their midst to save them. We have an amazing GOD.

I remember thinking a few years back that "mas" in Spanish means "more". May we all have a blessed CHRIST-MAS by having MORE Christ in our hearts.

PRAYER FOR THE BLESSING OF THE DAY...

On this day of Your Holy Birth, and Jesus, we bless You and thank You. We are so grateful that You became a child of our world so we could become children of Heaven. AMEN.

Fr. Dale

December 26

ONE LESSON I HAVE LEARNED IN MY LIFE IS...

I am responsible for my own happiness. I have the power to make great things happen, be in charge of good decisions, and stay in a positive mindset. I can choose to: (a) wake up in the morning and be grateful for a new and blessed day; (b) start each day with a fresh new attitude and give more than you take and, (c) In the evening, count all the positive things that happened -- even if they are simple things like helping someone, doing a good deed, or having a great lunch with a friend. Sharing your blessings can make and keep you happy and can spread to others.

God wants for us to be happy. He gave us life so that we could love and be loved. He gave each and every one of us gifts so that we may share those gifts and be happy. Finding happiness in the simple things is a great blessing. Sharing our happiness can fill others with joy.

PRAYER FOR THE BLESSING OF THE DAY...

(Mother Teresa)

"People who love each other fully and truly are the happiest people in the world. They may have little, they may have nothing, but they are happy people. Everything depends on how we love one another."

Lord, help me remember the words of Mother Teresa. AMEN.

Cindy A. Kiraly

December 27

ONE LESSON I HAVE LEARNED IN MY LIFE IS...

The week between Christmas and New Year's can truly be the "most wonderful time of the year." The rush is over, the decorations are still up, and there are more opportunities to visit with family and friends who are home for the holidays.

Christmas is a season, and not a single day.

PRAYER FOR THE BLESSING OF THE DAY...

Lord, let me savor every bit of the meaning of Christmas. Encourage me to listen to the music with new ears, and to keep from rushing through the celebration of the birth of Your son. Help me embrace all the colors and textures of this special time of year to remember for times when joy feels far very away.

Jody Serey

December 28

ONE LESSON I HAVE LEARNED IN MY LIFE IS...

There is a difference between believing in God and following God. The high percentage of Americans that say they believe is much different than the low percentage of people who surrender to God's will.

In a book called A Trip Around the Sun, author Mark Batterson says his life changed when, "...his prayers became less about telling God what I wanted Him to do for me and more about asking what I could do for Him."

The real spiritual journey happens when we put God in control of our lives. All I know is my way isn't working so well. His way is much better.

PRAYER FOR THE BLESSING OF THE DAY...

Jesus, I surrender to You. I give You control of my life. Use me as You wish. I trust You, Jesus.

Fr. Dale

December 29

ONE LESSON I HAVE LEARNED IN MY LIFE IS...

God is the Alpha and the Omega. Like you, I've heard that expression many times. And to be honest with you, I have never given it much thought. God says it very clearly in the book of Revelation (21:6), "I am the Alpha and the Omega, the beginning and the end."

The expression itself comes from the Greek alphabet. Alpha is the first letter. Omega is the last. So in other words, He is telling us, I am the beginning and I am the end.

What difference does that make? Well, we know how the world starts and we know who wins in the end. And that makes all the difference in the world. If you sat down to watch a football game and you knew the final score, you would watch the game in a different way. You would understand each play, or each call by a referee doesn't matter quite so much because your team WINS when it is all over. As Christians, we care about our world. But we also know that in the end, God defeats evil. Nobody who lies, cheats, or steals wins. We know the end of the story.

We live by faith in this life, knowing that God's judgment and justice will always have the final say. And it is right that He should. He is the Creator and He is the one who is victorious in the end.

PRAYER FOR THE BLESSING OF THE DAY...

(Revelation 1:8)

"Look! He is coming with the clouds; Every eye will see Him, Even those who pierced him: On His account all the tribes of the earth will wail. So it is to be. AMEN.

'I am the Alpha and the Omega' says the Lord God, who is and who was and who is to come, the Almighty."

Fr. Dale

December 30

ONE LESSON I HAVE LEARNED IN MY LIFE IS...

Working on this devotional for Father Dale has been a pleasure. It has been a wonderful blessing to "walk" through the prayers, thoughts and feelings of the community. Through this devotional we have all seen that God is with us and in us throughout each day. He is with us in our ups and downs and doesn't leave us.

Hopefully we have all come away this year as a stronger person of faith. Hopefully next year we will all be more faithful and continue growing in Christ.

PRAYER FOR THE BLESSING OF THE DAY...

Lord, help us to continue to grow in faith and love with You each and every day in the New Year. Revitalize us through prayer, worship and service to one another.

Guide our pastors, deacons and interns to help us come closer to You. AMEN.

Stephanie Rehm

December 31

ONE LESSON I HAVE LEARNED IN MY LIFE IS...

Always believe we will make next year better than this last year. And although there are many things we have no control over (economy, world events, natural disasters), there are some things we can work on. Here is a list of 10 suggestions from me:

(1) Stay close to God.

(2) Say "I love you" more often.

(3) Laugh more.

(4) Try to get out of debt.

(5) Be kinder to others and yourself.

(6) Learn something new.

(7) Eat healthier.

(8) Do something specific to grow spiritually.

(9) Be less judgmental of others.

(10) Rearrange something in your house.

May we all have a blessed New Year.

PRAYER FOR THE BLESSING OF THE DAY...

May the Lord bless us and keep us.

May the Lord let His light shine upon us.

May the Lord look upon us kindly,

And give us His peace.

AMEN.

Fr. Dale

www.ingramcontent.com/pod-product-compliance
Lightning Source LLC
Chambersburg PA
CBHW030529100426
42813CB00001B/199